GAY ICONS

GAY ICONS

Introduction by Sandi Toksvig
Essay by Richard Dyer

National Portrait Gallery, London

Published in Great Britain by National Portrait Gallery Publications, National Portrait Gallery, St Martin's Place, London WC2H 0HE

Published to accompany the exhibition *Gay Icons* held at the National Portrait Gallery, London, from 2 July to 18 October 2009.

For a complete catalogue of current publications, please write to the National Portrait Gallery at the address above, or visit our website www.npg.org.uk/publications

ISBN: 978 185514 400 2

A catalogue record for this book is available from the British Library.

Publishing Manager: Celia Joicey
Project Editor: Rebeka Cohen
Production: Ruth Müller-Wirth
Design: True North
Printed in Italy

Front covers: Joe Dallesandro (detail), Paul Morrissey, 1968. Private Collection; k.d. lang (detail), Jill Furmanovsky, 1992. Jill Furmanovsky/www.rockarchive.com

Frontispiece: Quentin Crisp (detail), Fergus Greer, 1989. National Portrait Gallery, London (NPG x126805)

Gay Icons has been sponsored by

Rosé d'Anjou wines are worth savouring, please enjoy them responsibly.

D·RINKAWARE.CO.UK

CONTENTS

SPONSOR'S FOREWORD

The Loire wine producers of Rosé d'Anjou wines are delighted and proud to be the sponsor of the *Gay Icons* exhibition at the National Portrait Gallery, London.

Portraiture is an art form that is easy to relate to, cutting across racial, social, educational and economic barriers; it enhances cultural appreciation and awareness. Viticulture shares many of the same values – it blends grape varieties, personalities and cultures to create wines that are designed to be enjoyed in a diverse number of ways. We believe that our wines perfectly complement this exhibition because the wines appeal to a broad range of wine drinkers from every walk of life.

Rosé d'Anjou is a salmon-coloured, off-dry rosé wine produced by winemakers from around Angers in France's Loire Valley. A versatile and accessible wine, it is perfect with a whole range of foods and is excellent to slowly sip when contemplating great art.

We are sure that the *Gay Icons* exhibition will encourage a wide audience to think about familiar faces in new ways, and we hope our wines will surprise and delight in a similar manner.

Olivier Lecomte
President
Rosé d'Anjou Syndicate

DIRECTOR'S FOREWORD

'Gay Icons' is a title of some creative ambiguity. For many the term will refer to well-known historical or literary figures, such as Oscar Wilde, who have become iconic through their status as pioneers or even martyrs. For others it will signify those stars like Judy Garland, Madonna or Kylie Minogue who have developed a cult status for a gay audience because of their style or appearance. For this project, the term is extended to include those people, living or dead, whatever their sexual orientation or interests, who our ten individual selectors regard as inspirational as a personal icon. *Gay Icons* therefore brings together an intriguing set of portraits: those people who are regarded as especially significant by each of the selectors, alongside the selectors themselves, who are prominent gay figures in contemporary culture and society.

This book and the exhibition it accompanies are assertive, exploratory and celebratory. The choices of iconic figures and their portraits provide a fascinating range of inspiring figures – some very famous, some heroic, others not sufficiently well-known. Each subject is presented along with information about their personal, and sometimes public, significance. Some of it relating to the sitter but much of it linked to the selectors themselves. This makes for some poignant and unexpected juxtapositions: in writing about their choices, the selectors have been prepared to share their own experiences and feelings, which in turn raises issues about gender, identity, history and iconography for wider consideration.

The project was developed from an initial proposal made by Bernard Horrocks, Copyright Officer at the Gallery, which was welcomed with enthusiasm by the Exhibitions Committee. The concept quickly evolved to include invitations to ten gay people – each distinguished in different fields – to act as selectors. This selection of the selectors was made with the help of the Chair, Sandy Toksvig. Each selector could freely choose six 'icons', although the Gallery had decided to limit the choices to photographic portraits, and therefore to subjects who had lived, more or less, within the last 150 years. This seemed appropriate because it has been within this same period that homosexuality has become more socially established, and homosexual relationships gradually accepted and made legitimate in Britain.

My sincere thanks go to all the selectors – Waheed Alli, Alan Hollinghust, Elton John, Jackie Kay, Billie Jean King, Ian McKellen, Chris Smith, Ben Summerskill, Sandi Toksvig and Sarah Waters – for creating this exhibition and book and collaborating with us in the shaping of its contents. I would also like to thank Mary McCartney for her beautiful portraits of the selectors. Thanks are also due to the lenders of the photographs to the exhibition, and to those who have helped in the research and the locating of these images. I am particularly grateful to Bernard Horrocks for proposing the idea and, together with Peter Funnell, advising as it developed. Sandi Toksvig has been an excellent Chair of the selectors, and essayist too. My thanks go to her and to Robert Jones for his work on the exhibition design, and especially to Richard Dyer for his exposition of the development of the terminology of gay icons.

The whole project has been skilfully overseen at the National Portrait Gallery by Pim Baxter, Deputy Director and Communications and Development Director, and I should like to thank her for all her hard work and commitment. Pim has been supported by Rosie Wilson, Exhibitions Manager, and by Rebeka Cohen, Editor, and I am grateful to them. I should also like to thank Andrea Easey, Denise Ellitson, Neil Evans, Caroline Hawley, Celia Joicey, Ruth Müller-Wirth, Christa Munns, Jonathan Rowbotham, Jude Simmons, Liz Smith, Sarah Tinsley, Helen Trompeteler and Helen Whiteoak, and all the National Portrait Gallery staff who have contributed to the exhibition and publication.

I should also like to extend warm thanks to a number of individual supporters, and most particularly to the Loire wine producers of Rosé d'Anjou wines as sponsor of the exhibition, and to Olivier Lecomte, President of the Rosé d'Anjou Syndicate.

Sandy Nairne
Director
National Portrait Gallery, London

INTRODUCTION

Sandi Toksvig

Occasionally one of the more thoughtful newspapers in Britain decides they ought to nod in the direction of gay culture. They produce a list, usually called something pompous like 'The Most Influential Gay People in Britain', in which they attempt to rank gay people into some kind of success table. If the editors are feeling they need a bit more colour then they combine gays and money with an article along the lines of 'The Pink Pound People'. This suggests a financially fortunate gay subculture, but also has a pleasingly camp ring to it.

For the rest of the time gay people are, in terms of the mainstream media, often pretty invisible. Ask a viewer about a lesbian moment on television and they will probably have to hark back to 1993 when actress Anna Friel famously had a sapphic kiss on *Brookside*. When *EastEnders* showed its first gay male kiss back in 1987 it was a peck on the forehead, which earned the soap opera the tabloid headline '*Eastbenders*'. Questions were asked in parliament and there were calls for the programme to be banned. Nine years later the *EastEnders*' bosses cut a kiss between two men from two seconds to half a second because they didn't want to 'startle' viewers.

When it comes to the cinema things get worse. Take the film *Notes on a Scandal*: based on a book by Zoë Heller, the 2006 film seeks disappointing refuge in every possible stereotype for the single, older lesbian. In it the main character, Barbara Covett, ticks every box available. Of course she is a teacher in charge of vulnerable youth; of course she has a cat, no one likes her, she lives alone and of course she has 'unnatural'

feelings for her younger colleague, which border on the psychotic. You certainly don't have to be gay to write about it, but you do have the sense that Ms Heller's closest contact with the gay world was a single dance to Village People's 'YMCA' in her youth. It was as though modern culture had moved nowhere at all since the 1964 play *The Killing of Sister George* in which the main character, June Buckridge, is a successful actress by day and a closeted lesbian by night. Not just any lesbian either. Naturally the strain of her sexuality means that she swills gin, chomps cigars and has a sadistic streak to boot. Where are the stories of the well-functioning homosexual couples, often with children, who just get on with their lives? Well, not in the mainstream media at any rate.

The latest Whitehall estimates from 2005 show there are about 3.6 million gay people living in the UK.[1] That's quite a big minority group to be so soundly and relentlessly both under- and misrepresented. Things, of course, have improved. There are now civil partnerships and it is possible to be both out and still working in the mainstream media, but it is rare. Sadly, I know of far more frightened and closeted public figures than I do contented and out ones.

There are several reasons for this ongoing fear of acceptance. One is the continuing homophobia in many of the main world religions. For example, the Anglican church, in theory a place to find love and comfort, has made it quite clear that homosexuals are to blame for tearing the church apart. The earth is in a parlous state and one might have thought Anglicans had better things to do such as charitable acts, but instead they focus on condemning gay people in this life as a prelude to hell and damnation in the next.

I believe secrets are a cancer of the soul and prefer to live out and proud with my head held high. However, in order to do so, everyone, whatever the path they walk in life, needs inspirational figures. The historic lack of positive gay role models has not made it easy for the young homosexual person to identify with a future life in which they can be comfortable both with themselves and with society.

When I was growing up in the 1960s I knew that I had strong feelings for my best friend, but absolutely nothing told me this might end happily in a committed relationship. All I knew was that of *Janet and John* I always thought John had more fun. It must be hard for heterosexuals to imagine growing up in a world where every advertisement, every book and every film seem to have nothing to do with their first fledgling feelings.

This dearth of representation makes it even more remarkable that some people have chosen to live their lives with their heads above the parapet. You have to wonder what inspired them to think that leading a life outside the pale would be a good choice in a world where Radio 1 disc jockeys use the word 'gay' to mean 'rubbish' or 'stupid' and opinion polls show that twenty-five per cent of the UK population believe that homosexual sex should be re-criminalised.[2]

When the ten selectors for the *Gay Icons* exhibition put in their selection of sixty inspirational figures there were quite a few expressions of

surprise. Where was Oscar Wilde? What about Radclyffe Hall? Surely someone should have nodded to Michelangelo or Alexander the Great? Who could possibly have left out a nudge to Shakespeare or Leonardo da Vinci? Heavens, hadn't anyone heard the rumours about Florence Nightingale? All right, at least some divas needed to be there – Barbra Streisand, Cher, Kylie? Liza Minnelli, for goodness' sake.

The fact is the choices were all intensely personal. Each of the selectors comes from the gay community; although to be honest, I don't really know what that means. It makes it sound as though gay people have their own village hall where they get together, presumably with village people, and share insights into musical theatre. Just being gay is probably not enough to make a minority into a community. Just like straight people, homosexuals present themselves in many guises. If they have anything in common it is that life will not always have been easy.

Personally I don't believe that being gay is a choice. Falling in love is about the release of chemicals in the body and I doubt many people have full command of their pheromones. No one can choose when they get that lump in the throat and rush of excitement that comes with finding a partner. What they can choose is what they do about it. Each of the selectors is a successful person in their own right who also happens to be gay. Their lives in the public eye will not have been made easier by their decision to live openly with their sexuality. Dealing with, at best, gossip and, at worst, derision or even death threats (usually from the evangelically religious) is not unusual. I, myself, am on kissing terms with the police hate crime squad and often think what an odd thing it is to be reviled by someone simply for being yourself. Finding out who helped to give our selectors the courage to stand tall is fascinating, for their choices do not reflect what anyone could have predicted.

Every decision for the exhibition was entirely personal. Without any interference each of our ten selectors selected the six people to whom they wanted to point as having been important or influential to them. Most significantly, the choices themselves are not necessarily gay. Being a gay icon doesn't mean you have to be homosexual yourself. You need to be something even rarer – you need to be inspirational. You need to be someone a gay person can point to and say 'somehow they made things easier for me'.

People such as Billie Jean King's parents and brother, who helped her personally, and the bookseller Jane Cholmeley, who, with her Silver Moon bookshop, helped a generation of women. The list includes those willing to risk their own lives to stand up for others: men such as Bishop Gene Robinson, Harvey Milk and Peter Tatchell; activists such as Angela Mason and Sojourner Truth; and the downright bold such as Colonel Margarethe Cammermeyer, the highest ranking US military official to come out while in service to her country.

There are many people on the list who even the most conscientious broadsheet editor would fail to include in their 100 Great Gay Icons. Take for example the Caribbean-American writer, poet and activist Audre Lorde. I wonder how many non-academics in the UK are aware of her? She believed we should celebrate our diversity and not try to lump people into

sustainable categories that work well only for statisticians. As she once said, 'If I didn't define myself for myself, I would be crunched into other people's fantasies for me and eaten alive'.

The list also prompts us to reconsider celebrated names such as Daphne Du Maurier, who struggled with her sexuality to the extent that she felt she had a split personality – her public side being the loving wife and mother while privately a decidedly male demon of desire fuelled her creativity. W.H. Auden's fascination with political and economic unrest was ignited in 1920s Berlin. He might never have gone there had he not been seeking a city where homosexuality was less repressed than in his homeland.

There are many on the list whose own sexuality is utterly irrelevant compared to the influence of their work, such as: Mstislav Rostropovich, the Russian cellist and conductor, who fought for art without borders and freedom of speech; Walt Whitman, the American poet of democracy; and the unsung Hilda Matheson, who founded Radio 4 as we know it today.

The real wonder of this list is that it was ever reduced down to sixty. It is easy to become a little morose about the frequent failure of modern culture to portray people in all the many guises in which they present themselves. How I wish this selection had been available to me when I was young and trying to make sense of my reactions to the world. How inspirational to have had portraits of the great and the good staring out at me telling me that I was not by any measure on my own.

As Audre Lorde said, 'It is not our differences that divide us. It is our inability to recognise, accept, and celebrate those differences'. Well, here is a celebration: a great celebration of great gay icons, and about time too.

NOTES
1 UK Department of Trade and Industry, Final Regulatory Impact Assessment: Civil Partnership Act, 2004.

2 The *Observer* Sex Poll, 26 October 2008.

THE IDEA OF A GAY ICON

Richard Dyer

In 1882 Oscar Wilde, newly arrived in the USA, had his portrait taken by one of the most important photographers of the day, Napoleon Sarony (below left). He was to use the images to advertise his tour, which is to say himself, but they were also very widely circulated, unauthorised, by the Burrow-Giles Lithographic Company.[1] Wilde was already famous, if not quite yet infamous, but in relatively limited circles. The photographs made him familiar to the masses. Wilde's look in these photos, to which Sarony as well as Wilde himself contributed – the longish hair, velvet jacket and silk stockings, the languid poses, the Turkish carpet and hangings – fixed and spread the idea not only of Wilde but of a type that may not quite have spoken its name yet, but was widely recognised or suspected. Wilde was, literally, the embodiment of a known social category, captured in a photograph. In other words, he was a gay icon.[2]

It may feel heart-sinkingly predictable to introduce an introduction to gay iconography with Oscar Wilde – yet it is precisely that predictability, that excessive familiarity, which makes him so inescapably a gay icon. This is true even if historical investigation should make us worry about just how entirely gay he was (there is no reason to suppose he did not also love, sexually, his wife and other women) and quite how many people knew that his floppy, foppish look meant homosexual (rather than just weird). Wilde to some extent was and certainly has become an icon, a person who is taken to be an embodiment of a wider social category and who is known about through the mass reproduction of, supremely, photographic images of him or her; and in Wilde's case the social category is the homosexual. Before, and even long after, Wilde's trial and disgrace in 1895, when the love that dare not speak its name or show its face had had that done for it decisively by the law and the press, no one would have actually used the term gay icon. Even thirty years ago it would have meant very little. Icon, if it meant anything, meant an image of Christ or the Virgin Mary or, more arcanely, visual symbolism in art[3] or a kind of sign designated within the fledgling discipline of semiotics.[4] Gay as a term designating homosexual was gaining ground, although it would certainly have meant nothing in this regard to the Victorians (or to many people before the 1960s), who had at their disposal venerable terms such as pederast and sodomite, lesbian and sapphic, nelly and molly and tommy, and emergent ones such as invert, uranian and homosexual. The idea of putting any of those terms together with icon would have appeared baffling. Their coming together in the past thirty years is a product of the separate but intertwined establishment of the two terms, gay and icon, in their homosexual and semiotic senses. This though is not mere coincidence, for the term gay was part of a project about making homosexuality visible and icons are one of the main forms of doing this in contemporary mass media. There were images of people relatively widely known to be gay – or lesbians, or queers, or homosexuals – before there was the word gay, but the business of making gay icons is largely a product of recent times. That doesn't mean, however, that it isn't revealing to think about the implications of both halves of the term – icon and gay – in relation to their earlier meanings and connotations.

Oscar Wilde, 1854–1900
Napoleon Sarony, 1882
Albumen panel print,
305 x 184mm (12 x 7¼")
National Portrait Gallery,
London (NPG P25)

The religious meaning of the term icon, and the adoption of it for semiotic purposes, is not negligible. The religious icon is part of a fundamental distinctiveness of Christianity, the idea of embodiment. Christ was the embodiment of God, and the Virgin bore Him in her body (there is no such embodiment in Judaism, and Mohammed is always referred to as the Prophet or Messenger, not God incarnate). Although Christian icons are only images, they are images of persons who stand for a much wider (in this case the very widest possible) category. What's more they don't just stand for it, they are it; in their very persons, they incarnate it. The idea of embodiment and its image has transmuted into the secular world, and the term icon is now very widely used to mean a person or a thing that at once stands for and is a representative of a wider category. In writing this essay, I have become especially aware of how wholly commonplace a term it has become with, for instance, fashion items, films and cities, as well as people routinely referred to as iconic (sometimes without even an indication as to what they are iconic of). It may also include fictional people – in the present context Dorian Gray, Elsie Tanner from *Coronation Street*, Colin in *EastEnders*, Willow in *Buffy the Vampire Slayer*, and Xena in *Xena: Warrior Princess* are examples of iconic fictional gay characters. However, its primary meaning, even in secular use and the one deployed here, still has to do with real people who embody a wider category.

The secularisation of the term is related in part to the challenge to belief in the West during the past centuries and also to the

transformation of Christianity into a religion of the here and now rather than of the hereafter (a transformation surfacing in celebrity culture in all those awards ceremonies where no doubt iconic people candidly thank God for their celebrity). It also has to do with the profound effect of two things that are at once wholly comprehensible and yet, at least for a time, seemingly uncanny, like the idea of embodiment itself: the mass circulation of images and photography. The first (in the form of woodblocks, engravings and lithographs in broadsheets, chapbooks and newspapers, long before the advent of photography) made images of people available on a hitherto unimaginably wide scale. A painted portrait – let us say for the sake of the present context of Shakespeare's patron, Henry Wriothesley (above right), widely taken to be homosexual – may have captured the image of someone whose being embodied a certain orientation, and both the person and the portrait may have been well enough known in certain circles to make the person a byword for said orientation. Those circles, however, would be very restricted indeed – really only a few people would ever have seen the portrait of Wriothesley at the time and only with the possibility of reproduction has it become widely known. It is the mass circulation of infinitely reproducible images that made it possible for a private individual's likeness to be known to all and sundry, made icons in the contemporary mass-media sense possible.

The uncanniness of the photographic portrait is that it derives technically from the subject's actual presence in front of the camera.[5] A lithograph of

Henry Wriothesley, 3rd Earl of Southampton, 1573–1624 (detail)
After Daniel Mytens, c1618?
Oil on canvas, 889 × 686mm (35 × 27")
National Portrait Gallery, London (NPG 52)

The Ladies of Llangollen
Lady Eleanor Charlotte Butler, 1745?–1829, and Sarah Ponsonby, 1755?–1831
James Henry Lynch, 1887
Lithograph, 323 × 219mm (12¾ × 8⅝")
National Portrait Gallery, London (NPG D14047)

Radclyffe Hall (Marguerite Antonia
Radclyffe Hall), 1880–1943 (detail)
Howard Coster, 1932
Half-plate film negative,
191 x 240mm (7½ x 9½")
National Portrait Gallery,
London (NPG x10422)

someone – in the case at hand, that of the Ladies of Llangollen (who died just when photography was being invented) is a good example (below right) – made the image of the person available to all, but it was still just someone's impression of them and could even have been made up, whereas a photograph can only exist if the person was there to be photographed. But, like a lithograph only more so as the media of mass reproduction developed, a photograph could be seen by thousands and millions. The photograph then is the means for the mass circulation of embodiment and may even make it possible for an individual person to be taken as an embodiment of a wider category, in other words, to be an icon.[6] Mass reproduction and photography are utterly routine now: we don't find them uncanny. And yet something of the extraordinary remains, of a particular person whose appearance can be captured and seen anywhere over and over again; this extraordinariness is part of the process of icon-making, of ordinary people becoming special.

The religious connotation of the word icon does not stop at its semiotic function, but also relates to its lingering extraordinariness. The prime purposes of religious icons are devotion and veneration. In some traditions they are even themselves considered to be endowed with actual godhead, just as the communion wafer commonly is in Catholic tradition. We may not go as far as this with gay icons (although something akin to it is possible), but they generally function as something more than a convenient reference point for homosexuality in image communication. On the one hand, while the person concerned may be ordinary, typical, just like you

and me, they are also at the same time special. They are special partly just because they are icons, but then they generally become icons because in some way or other they have done or been something special (see below). On the other hand, what these people have done is generally for the most part something admirable or likeable. There are infamous lesbians and gay men (beyond those infamous in their own time just for being gay, such as Wilde or Radclyffe Hall (left)), but can they ever quite be gay icons? Can one imagine Gilles de Rais, Erzsébet Báthory, Ernst Röhm, Roy Cohn, Dennis Nilsen or Jeffrey Dahmer – who have high name and even image recognition – figuring in a gay icons listing or exhibition? In other words, can one have, in the old negative sense of the term, a queer icon? And even less in the more recent radical use of the term queer, which stresses fluidity and destabilisation, whereas icons are fixed as well as positive.

All of which brings me to the significance of the other half of the term under discussion: gay. The word was part of a project that saw the road to rights and equality for people who desired people of the same sex in terms of a visible identity. The gay project was carried vocally in the activities of the Gay Liberation Front and associated movements, but also in the more respectable activity of homosexual rights groups, as well as in the practices of stereotyping in the mass media, which, for their own various purposes – responding, denigrating, taking possession of representation – wanted gays to be recognisable. Informal and vernacular as it is, at once subcultural and mass-media based, the production of gay icons is carrying on the gay liberation project of coming out and becoming visible.

Making gayness visible had to overcome the fact that, apart from actual sexual acts, homosexuality is not something visible, something that can be seen (or of course heard, but we'll stick to the visible for the purposes of this discussion). There had already been a history of queer-spotting – could you tell who was and who wasn't? Were all women wearing ties in the 1920s lesbian? How sure a giveaway were suede shoes for men in the 1960s? But the gay project wanted a more secure visibility, it wanted to make widespread the face, literally, of homosexuality.

The problem is that once you have a recognisable image, you are in the business of fixing an identity, of saying this is what a lesbian or a gay man looks like and this is what they are like. Many gay icons affirm this – you probably didn't need to know that Wilde, Hall, Martina Navratilova (p.89) or Little Richard were gay to be able to guess as much from their images. Which is to say they affirm stereotypes. The latter are often taken to be simplistic, reductive and derogatory and, in the case of lesbian and gay stereotypes, they tend to reinforce the sense of homosexuality being a form of gender dissonance (we are not real men and women).

Yet these stereotypes do not simply go away. They are a very effective and immediate form of communication, all the more powerfully so for invisible groups (like homosexuals), and they are at least as much a product of lesbian and gay communities as something imposed upon them. Yet the gay project remained uneasy about stereotypes: they were used against us, they did imply that all homosexuals were like this or that, were gender misfits and, if we acted

them out, maybe that was a mark of our oppression, of our internalisation of the way we were seen by straights. Gay icons – when they are real gay people taken to be representative of gay people in general – in some measure, if they aren't themselves 'obvious' dykes and poofs, evade this problem. If you didn't know they were gay you couldn't tell just from looking, but such gay icons by definition are proclaimed or proclaim themselves as gay, so that you always do know that this unexceptional looking person signifies that exceptional thing, gay.

There remains though a further ambiguity over gay icons, whether partaking of stereotypicality or not. Something of this ambiguity derives from the nature of the portrait itself. Gay icons do not only exist in portraiture of course; they exist in their publicly recognised activity, in performances, interviews, audio-visual footage and so on. However, it is not just the relevance of portraiture in the present context that makes me raise it here. Albeit not necessarily in posed and/or photographic form, the portrait remains a privileged mode in gay iconography, precisely because it fixes an immediately recognisable and readily reproducible image of its subject. In the process it carries the ambiguity of the social function of portraiture. Before the Renaissance, and really for long after, portraits were of rulers, religious leaders, kings, queens, popes, the nobility, the rich and powerful – while no doubt the portraits of Richard I (above right) or Queen Anne (below right) – to take once again subjects germane to the topic of gay icons – were of interest because they told viewers what this king and this queen looked like, they were primarily significant because they were The King or

Richard I ('the Lionheart'), 1157–99
Probably by Renold or Reginold
Elstrack (Elstracke), 1618
Line engraving, 172 x 111mm (6¾ x 4⅜")
National Portrait Gallery,
London (NPG D32012)

Queen Anne, 1665–1714
Sir Godfrey Kneller, Bt. c.1690
Oil on canvas, 2337 x 1429mm (92 x 56¼")
National Portrait Gallery,
London (NPG 1616)

Una, Lady Troubridge, 1887–1963
Romaine Brooks, 1924
Oil on canvas,
1273 x 764mm (50⅛ x 30⅛")
Smithsonian American Art Museum

The Queen. Only gradually did the portrait become specifically of an individual. With icons, something of the old function remains – the person is significant as themselves but also as lesbian or gay or as being important to the lesbian or gay community, at once themselves as individuals and representative, with the latter always risking sliding over into the vexed question of typicality.

A gay icon then, for the purposes of this discussion, is a widely known and disseminated visual image of a real person who is taken to be representative of the social category homosexual and to be in some way or other valued for it. From this follow the two elements that make a given person come to be considered a gay icon: visibility and representativeness.

A gay icon has to be visible, but this does not absolutely have to be in photographic form: Wilde may well have been visible first in newspaper cartoons and Radclyffe Hall's partner Una Troubridge is iconic in Romaine Brooks's (much reproduced) painting of her (left). Photography, however, is overwhelmingly the medium of choice in gay icon-making, not least for its affirmation, as discussed above, of the person's existence (and an urgent aim of the gay project was to proclaim the very existence of lesbians and gay men).

Of course if one were to include people who lived before the invention of photography, one would have to resort to pre-photographic sources of imagery. In this essay I have deliberately, for the purposes of historical perspective and resonance, gone beyond the photographic remit of the exhibition it accompanies, but two cautions are in order. The first and simpler of these is

that the making of icons is only possible by means of photography, though in the case of people before there was photography, this means photographs of their images in painting and other non-mechanically reproducible media. Gay icons must be represented in images that are widely available and this is only possible by means of photography and its derivatives. Secondly, and more complicatedly, the very idea of making icons belongs overwhelmingly, as I am arguing, to the past twenty-odd years: it is a product of the age of gayness and celebrity. Nominating people as icons from earlier, non-gay times (including those captured in photographs) runs a number of risks. Firstly, it will involve making into icons figures who, with a number of remarkable exceptions (for example, Byron, the Ladies of Llangollen), had no such public position in their own time – it is us now who make them into icons. People with same-sex desires in the past no doubt had their own icons, ambivalently valued for their homosexuality, but these would have only been known in very restricted circles. Now we may rescue queers, or same-sex lovers, of the past from their own ambivalence and opprobrium and see them as gay icons.

Secondly, nominating people from the past as gay icons may be profoundly anachronistic. Not only was the term gay not available, but nor – perhaps, sometimes – was the idea of people being of a specific sexuality or having a particular sexual identity.

Thirdly, even if we are careful to think in terms of 'people who had same-sex loves' rather than of gays *avant la lettre*, we are usually caught up in hints and conjectures, since the hard evidence is rarely to be found. Especially difficult is the language of friendship in previous times, often passionate and physical without necessarily connoting sexuality. This is extraordinarily difficult territory to negotiate. For, just as we should not seek to impose our ideas of gayness onto the past, nor should we assume that because there weren't the words and it was all hints and conjectures that we are not justified in claiming any gay icons at all from the past. There is a tension here between the actual contemporary practice of establishing a pantheon of gay icons and the work of lesbian and gay historians; between, that is, the activity of lesbians and gay men now who appropriate people as gay as they will (and as is their inalienable right) and the historians' quite proper fastidiousness concerning accuracy and the use of today's categories to read back into the past. Sappho, for instance, though widely revered in the ancient world, is almost an invention. Very little of her work survived, and what little we know suggests she had male lovers as well as passionate female friendships. Yet we would not want to renounce her as – now – a lesbian icon, nor could we: her place in the iconographic pantheon is a fact of our cultural life.

Gay icons may have to be made visible. Some may have to be rescued from the obscurity of the past. Alan Turing (p.83), widely regarded as the inventor of the computer and thus perhaps one of the most influential people of the past century, was nonetheless in his lifetime hardly known at all outside of the world of mathematics, much less as gay (except to those who attended his court prosecution for being gay, an event that did not receive significant publicity). Some people known at the time for their passionate attachments might have to be rediscovered and,

perhaps problematically, redefined as gay and made into gay icons: the bluestockings Elizabeth Carter (right) and Catherine Talbot, for instance, featured in the National Portrait Gallery's recent Brilliant Women exhibition.[7] Others, splendidly notorious in their day, get forgotten, such as the dancer Maud Allan, famous for various Salomé dances and a libel case caused by an article entitled 'The Cult of the Clitoris', which (rightly) insinuated her lesbianism. Some – Lord Kitchener, Marguerite Yourcenar – would almost certainly have been uncomfortable with their private life having the public presence necessary for iconicity. Yet others – A.E. Housman, Daphne Du Maurier (p.105), Gerard Manley Hopkins (p.40) – disliked the fact they were gay and might be horrified to find themselves now yanked into the limelight of iconicity. In some cases, even what they looked like is speculative and tradition-based. The earliest surviving images of the supreme lesbian icon, Sappho, for instance, date from well after her death[8] and the earliest extant portrait of Richard I was made over 400 years after his death.

Others may be famous for what they produced and are well known to be gay but not for their visual image. This is particularly true of writers. If there are some who are iconic in image as well as in name – Wilde, Hall, Gertrude Stein, James Baldwin – many others are not (I'm not sure that I'd recognise with confidence photographs of Paul Verlaine, Langston Hughes or Marguerite Yourcenar). One of the most beloved gay artists, Tom of Finland (Touko Laaksonen), produced some of the most immediately recognisable of all gay erotic imagery, but few would recognise a photograph of him (in fact the only one in general

Elizabeth Carter, 1717–1806
Sir Thomas Lawrence, 1788–9
Pastel on vellum, 311 × 273mm (13¾ × 11⅝")
National Portrait Gallery, London (NPG 28)

circulation is by another gay icon many people would probably not recognise from his photograph, Robert Mapplethorpe). It is much easier for someone to be elected a gay icon if they are already visible, hence the predominance of figures from entertainment, sport and politics.

A gay icon has to be taken to represent a wider identity, gay. This does not mean that they have to be lesbian or gay themselves. They do not even need to be of the same sex. There is a long tradition among gay men of enthusiasm for certain kinds of women stars: as one gay icon reportedly said to another – Joe Orton (p.90) to Kenneth Williams (p.107) – one could always tell if a man was gay because he had lots of Judy Garland albums. It is possible to see such stars – Garland, Mina, Barbra Streisand, Shirley Bassey (opposite), Madonna – as expressing specific aspects of gay culture and existence, and one might trace a shift in the character of these stars from the emotional intensity of a Bette Davis or a Joan Crawford to the upbeat image of a Kylie Minogue, with Princess Diana (p.34) perhaps occupying a middle position in this trajectory. Such stars may be taken to express aspects of gay existence – and stereotypical terms such as excessive, theatrical and camp often spring to lips when they are mentioned – but in many ways it is the simple fact of the readiness of a group of men to feel that their feelings can be carried in the person of a woman whom they do not desire sexually that is distinctive, and which makes them into gay icons. There is a comparable taste among lesbians for certain kinds of male star, often glamorous transgressors or outsiders, often with ambiguous homosexual

associations. Terry Castle has written of the importance of 'Byronic posturing' in the 'self-fashioning' of many lesbians, including many themselves indubitably iconic (Anne Lister, Radclyffe Hall, Vita Sackville-West, Billy Tipton (p.58), Marianne Moore, Nancy Spain),[9] while a sort of soft butchness, Elvis Presley or James Dean,[10] for instance, has been linked to the image of stars such as Phranc and k.d. lang (p.94). Suggestive in this context is the work of writers such as Mary Renault, Marguerite Yourcenar and Patricia Highsmith (p.103) whose lesbianism, not itself unknown to contemporaries, might be registered in their taste for often hyper-masculine male gay or homoerotic protagonists (Renault and Alexander the Great, Yourcenar and Hadrian, Highsmith and Tom Ripley). All these examples, from Alexander to Kylie, often have some hint (or more) of homoeroticism in their lives and work and, even when this is not so, they trail the connotations of gay stereotyping vis-à-vis gender: they are in some way misfits in terms of femininity and masculinity, louder and stronger and more libidinous than women are supposed to be (even while dressed up to the nines in frocks or leotards), more soft and sensitive than men are supposed to be (even while glowering and well built).

When the person is of the same sex, to be a gay icon they do not have to be – or be known to be – gay. Here desire usually comes into play. There are, for instance, long traditions of lesbian attachment to opera divas,[11] film stars such as Greta Garbo and Marlene Dietrich[12] and forceful musical theatre stars such as Mary Martin, Ethel Merman, Julie Andrews and Barbra Streisand.[13] There are often rumours about such stars' own lesbianism, but this is not indispensable to their lesbian following. Most often though they are seen – here we go again – as in some sense androgynous or mannish: favoured divas were often those who took on the breeches roles in opera (I think of female passions I know of currently for Sarah Connolly in such parts), donned male clothes (Garbo and Dietrich, Martin as Peter Pan) or were commanding and even loud (vide Merman) in a way associated with masculinity. Similarly, it is the predominant association of sport – and developed muscles – with masculinity that makes many sportswomen likely lesbian icons, whether or not they are in fact lesbian.[14] (There is of course a further history to be written about whether sport is in reality more accommodating to lesbians – or out lesbians – to say nothing of why tennis has been so especially lesbian identified: think Althea Gibson (p.65), Billie Jean King (p.60), Martina Navratilova (p.89), Chris Evert, Ilana Kloss (p.63), Amelie Mauresmo.) Such women are thus classic figures of homosexual desire, where the longing to have someone plays complexly with the yearning to be like them or even to be them (albeit not to the point of heterosexuality).

In contrast, gay men's icons of the same sex who are not (or may not) be gay do not, nowadays anyway, play on the borderline of male and female. There may be a felt affinity with the type of soft, troubled, even sad but not androgynous or, in any evident way, homosexual young man: James Dean, Keanu Reeves,[15] Johnny Depp. Just as – maybe even more – common are men who tend towards an excessive, theatricalised masculinity (musclemen, porn stars such as Joe Dallesandro (p.38) and Jeff Stryker (p.31)). With many male stars, and not least the porn stars,

the fact that they are not gay, or deny that they are, may even be part of the frisson of excitement.

Beyond such affinities and desires, the assumption or suspicion or just plain hope that someone is gay may be enough to make them a gay icon. People desired by the population as a whole are also going to be desired by lesbians and gay men. Think of the excitement surrounding Richard Gere, Jason Donovan and Tom Cruise, Mariel Hemingway, Catherine Deneuve, Dolly Parton and Madonna. The current Bollywood star Abhishek Bachchan has in recent polls been elevated to the status of gay icon and, in the wake of this, hopeful, or perhaps hopeless, rumours have circulated about his sexuality; in turn he has said how happy he would be to be a gay icon and has starred in what is seen as the first Bollywood gay movie, *Dostana* (Friendship), in which he and another major Hindi star, John Abraham, play two friends who pretend to be gay.

There are then many gay icons who are not themselves gay, nor even of the same sex as those for whom they are icons. However, having said all of that, it is probably the case that most gay icons are people who are known or presumed to be gay. This may be so even if they are also quite widely known to be, also, heterosexual: Byron, George Sand, Colette, Virginia Woolf (p.82), Bessie Smith (p.57), for instance, or, indeed, Sappho and Wilde. Or if they denied it, as Sarah Ponsonby and Eleanor Butler, and Walt Whitman (p.75) did. Or if in truth we don't really know – as is the case with those I casually recruited above: Richard I, Henry Wriothesley, Queen Anne, Elizabeth Carter and Catherine Talbot, as well as others regularly brought on board without cast-iron

Dame Shirley Bassey, b.1937
Mike Owen, 1997
Digital C-type colour print,
242 x 195mm (9½ x 7⅝")
National Portrait Gallery,
London (NPG x128532)

Rudolf Nureyev, 1938–93
Cecil Beaton, 1962
Vintage bromide print,
245 x 243mm (9⅝ x 9⅝")
National Portrait Gallery,
London (NPG x40301)

justification: Christopher Marlowe, Marie Antoinette, Franz Schubert, Alfred Lord Tennyson, cross-dressing women such as Moll Cutpurse and Mary Anne Talbot, let alone even less secure cases like William Shakespeare or Ethel Merman, for instance.

An especially interesting category of gay icons encompasses people that everyone in their circle knew to be gay, and from whom gossip leaked out to the wider pubic, and yet who were publicly known as straight. These are the kind of people of whom it is said nowadays that 'everyone knew,' but exactly who 'everyone' was in these cases remains uncertain. The list is interestingly long and distinguished, and includes Pyotr Ilyich Tchaikovsky (p.42), Selma Lagerlöf, Federico García Lorca, Vita Sackville-West, Ivor Novello, Langston Hughes, Billy Strayhorn, Noël Coward, Cecil Beaton, Benjamin Britten (p.80), Luchino Visconti, Dusty Springfield, Patricia Highsmith (p.103), John Cage, Rudolph Nureyev (left), Tove Jansson.

Lesbians and gay men in the 'everyone knew' category were in fact protected by it, since the 'everyone' who knew either didn't mind or weren't going to do anything about it. However, if they were forced out of such circles, they were at once vulnerable to public opprobrium and also on the way to becoming gay martyr-icons. Wilde and Hall are the obvious examples again, but another is furnished by the subject of a recent exhibition, the Victorian painter Simeon Solomon.[16] Everyone in his circle 'knew' and in any case his paintings told the story, but once arrested for importuning his career was finished. Later figures, in times of a greater flux in official public attitudes, have responded with courage, dignity and sense to the fact of exposure – John Gielgud,

George Michael – or the threat of it – Sandi Toksvig (p.93), Will Young (p.35). The last examples take us to what in practice is probably the core of gay iconicity: outness. On the whole, and with some sensitivity to the limitations on outness in previous eras, gay icons are gay people who, true to the gay project, are out as gay.

There are degrees of this and variations on it. The 'everyone knew' category is the half-open closet. Others were widely assumed to be gay because they conformed to a certain type recognised as gay: Herman Bang, Agnes Moorhead, Nancy Spain, Dirk Bogarde, Anthony Perkins, Elton John (p.45), Gianni Versace (p.46). Some are valued as openly gay even though their work is not – or not mainly – specifically to do with gayness: Ethel Smyth, Alan Turing (p.83), Andy Warhol, Angela Davis, Pat Arrowsmith, Waheed Alli (p.29), Alan Bennett, Matthew Parris, Miriam Margolyes, Maggi Hambling. Among others in this category are those who were the first openly lesbian or gay person in their field: the first (and in the event last) footballer, Justin Fashanu; the first American footballer, David Kopay; the first army colonel, Margarethe Cammermeyer (p.70); the first MPs (Chris Smith (p.77) and Angela Eagle); the first bishop, Gene Robinson (p.99).

Then there are those, in contrast, whose achievement is inextricable from, though not necessarily limited to, their gayness: Jean Cocteau, Noël Coward, W.H. Auden (p.79), Quentin Crisp (p.54), Joe Orton (p.90), Thom Gunn (p.43), Audre Lord (p.55), David Hockney (p.33), Elton John, Regina Fong (if drag is taken as an unmistakable sign of gay sensibility) (p.72), Larry Grayson, Rita Mae Brown, Derek Jarman, Alan Hollinghurst (p.36), Jackie Kay (p.53), Francis Bacon (p.88), Julian Clary (opposite), Paul O'Grady (even more than Lily Savage) (p.32), Matthew Bourne, Russell T. Davies, Sarah Waters (p.101).

The work of such people is openly coloured by their sexuality, which is not quite the same as those figures for whom proclaiming themselves gay (or whatever term they would have used at the time) was a conscious project: Radclyffe Hall, André Gide, Maureen Duffy, Ellen DeGeneres (p.87), Ian McKellen (p.69), and those firsts above, Fashanu, Cammermeyer, Chris Smith and Eagle, and then beyond them those who were actually activists, for whom being openly gay was itself a cornerstone of their work, before gay liberation (Edward Carpenter, Magnus Hirschfeld, Del Martin and Phyllis Lyon) and since (Michael Cashman, Peter Tatchell (p.98), Angela Mason, Harvey Milk (p.74), Ben Summerskill (p.857), Simon Nkoli).

The idea of gay icons is generous and inclusive, it makes available and celebrates a huge range of people. Yet, finally, one needs to register its limitations. Not everyone who has sex with someone of the same sex – and not even everyone who would consider themselves homosexual (and these two things are not the same – many who have sex with others of the same sex don't see themselves as homosexual) – recognises themselves in gay icons. While their sheer presence in the media may now incite many more people to see themselves in, and even model themselves on, such icons, my bet is that still the majority do not. Moreover, we need to remember how Western this concept is, and within that how disproportionately white, to say nothing of how slippery both I (here

and in the accompanying chronology) and the exhibition organisers have been about national and geographic scope. And the notion of a gay icon does not in practice centrally embrace all the constituents of sexual politics grouped under the current acronym, LGBT, lesbian, gay, bisexual and transgender.

Categories – such as gay icon – limit what is said, but they are also the means by which things are said and seen at all. The gay icon project values certain kinds of achievement, fixes images, often subtly reinforces stereotypes, makes being out a cardinal virtue, and is unconsciously constrained by being about current perceptions. However, it also makes possible a gay and lesbian public presence, contributes to changing attitudes and laws, and makes gayness familiar and available. Gay icons do what gay liberation wanted: they say to straights 'We're here' and to gays 'You're not alone'. Even ten years ago it was impossible to imagine an exhibition in as august an institution as the National Portrait Gallery on a declaredly lesbian or gay topic – for all the limitations of the very idea of gay icons, it is hard to think the very fact of an exhibition on them anything other than a gain.

Julian Clary, b.1959
Trevor Leighton, 1998
Bromide print, 301 x 1230mm (11⅞ x 9")
National Portrait Gallery,
Lodon (NPG x87779)

NOTES
1 For a discussion of the Sarony portraits and the Burrow-Giles appropriation of them, and the ensuing court case over copyright, see Jane Gaines, *Contested Culture: The Image, the Voice, and the Law* (University of North Carolina Press, Chapel Hill, 1991), pp.42–83.

2 In keeping with the terms of the exhibition I am using the term gay to cover both gay men and lesbians, a practice that only some lesbians will feel happy with.

3 See, for instance, Erwin Panofsky, *Meaning in the Visual Arts* (Doubleday, New York, 1955).

4 Namely one having meaning by virtue of its resemblance to what it represents. Thus a picture of something is understood to be a picture of that something because it looks like it, rather than because we agree to use an arbitrary sign to designate it or because the something itself causes the sign. Thus a picture of a cow looks like a cow, but the word cow is merely a convention by which English speakers designate the creature, and a cowpat is a sign of a cow because a cow itself created it. In this semiotic distinction, the first is an icon, the second a symbol and the third an index. Photography complicates the issue, as we shall see, because there is a sense in which the object photographed itself, by the virtue of light emanating from it being picked up and fixed on a light-sensitive surface, gives rise to the resultant photograph: outside of fakery and perhaps digitality, there can be no photograph without there having been the object in front of the camera to make it happen. However, we also understand a photograph to look like what it shows and it commonly has conventional associations beyond merely showing. Thus a photographic image is always an index and an icon and very often a symbol. The icon/index/symbol distinction belongs to the nineteenth-century philosopher C.S. Peirce; see James Hoopes (ed.), *Peirce on Signs* (University of North Carolina Press, Chapel Hill, 1991).

5 See previous note.

6 In Peircian terms an icon, in this cultural sense, gay or otherwise, is also an index (they are themselves a sign of what they are taken to represent and a photograph of them derives from their physical presence before the camera), a symbol (because much of what makes it possible to read them as anything other than that individual person is purely conventional, e.g. we have come to agree that a limp wrist 'means' queer, a tie on a woman 'suggests' lesbian) and rather more problematically an icon (since any individual lesbian or gay man does not in fact look like the generality of lesbians and gay men, even though they may be taken to do so).

7 National Portrait Gallery, London, 13 March to 15 June 2008; see Elizabeth Eger and Lucy Peltz, *Brilliant Women: 18th-Century Bluestockings* (National Portrait Gallery, London, 2008). On Carter and Talbot's relationship, see Lillian Faderman, *Surpassing the Love of Men: Romantic Friendship and Love Between Women from the Renaissance to the Present* (William Morrow, New York, 1981), pp.125–30.

8 See Dimitrios Yatromanolakis, *Sappho in the Making: The Early Reception* (Harvard University Press, Boston, 2007).

9 See Terry Castle, 'The Diaries of Anne Lister', *The Apparitional Lesbian: Female Homosexuality and Modern Culture* (Columbia University Press, New York, 1993), p.103.

10 On Dean as a lesbian icon, see Sue Golding, 'James Dean: the Almost-perfect Lesbian Hermaphrodite', *On Our Backs*, 1988, pp.18–9; 39–44.

11 See Terry Castle, 'In Praise of Brigitte Fassbaender (A Musical Emanation)', *The Apparitional Lesbian*, pp.200–38.

12 See Andrea Weiss, 'A Queer Feeling When I Look at You', *Stardom: Industry of Desire*, ed. Christine Gledhill (Routledge, London, 1991), pp.283–99.

13 See Stacy Wolf, *A Problem Like Maria: Gender and Sexuality in the American Musical* (University of Michigan Press, Ann Arbor, 2002).

14 On famous lesbian sportswomen – and indeed on lesbian celebrity in general – see Martha Gever, *Entertaining Lesbians: Celebrity, Sexuality, and Self-Invention* (Routledge, New York, 2003).

15 On Dean and Reeves in relation to gay imagery, see Michael De Angelis, *Gay Fandom and Crossover Stardom: James Dean, Mel Gibson, and Keanu Reeves* (Duke University Press, Durham, nc, 2001), which also discusses Gibson's brief period (that of the *Mad Max* films) of being a gay icon in the excessive, theatricalised masculinity mode before his determined repudiation of it.

16 See Colin Cruise et al. (eds), *Love Revealed: Simeon Solomon and the Pre-Raphaelites* (Merrell Publishers, London, 2005).

BC   **AD**

c.630/612–570
Life of Sappho, celebrated in her own time as one of the greatest poets, whose work extols the passions and pains of loving women.

399
Philosopher Socrates executed for the corruption of Athenian youth.

121
Publication of Suetonius' *The Lives of the Twelve Caesars*, in which he claims that the Emperor Nero was twice married to men.

130
The Emperor Hadrian begins commissioning statues and buildings in honour of his deceased beloved Antinous.

1440
German Johannes Gutenberg invents printing.

1780
Eleanor Butler and Sarah Ponsonby set up home in Llangollen, Wales, and become celebrated as the 'Ladies of Llangollen' (p.13).

1964/1968
Play and film of *The Killing of Sister George* (partially shot in the Gateways club).

1961
Release of film *Victim*, starring heart-throb Dirk Bogarde as a blackmailed homosexual lawyer.

1957
Publication of the Wolfenden Report, officially entitled the *Report of the Committee on Homosexual Offences and Prostitution*.

1955
Foundation of lesbian rights organisation Daughters of Bilitis in San Francisco.

1953
When he walks onstage in Liverpool, shortly after his court case for persistently importuning men for immoral purposes is splashed across the papers, John Gielgud receives a standing ovation.

1950
Foundation of the homosexual rights organisation the Mattachine Society in Los Angeles.

1966
Maureen Duffy publishes *The Microcosm*, an openly lesbian novel set in the lesbian club Gateways in Chelsea, London.

1967
Sexual Offences Act, 1967 passed in parliament, beginning the decriminalisation of homosexuality in the UK.

1969
Death of Judy Garland.

Riot at the Stonewall Inn, New York.

Foundation of Gay Liberation Front in New York.

1970
First meeting of Gay Liberation Front in London.

1972
Jackie Forster, a well-known broadcaster (under the name of Jacqueline Mackenzie), founds with some other women the group and magazine *Sappho*.

1977
The National Film Theatre in London, presents a season of thirty films dealing with 'Images of Homosexuality'. Questions are raised in the House of Lords over the use of public money.

2003
Openly gay minister Gene Robinson ordained Bishop in Durham, New Hampshire (p.99).

2002
Will Young, winner of the first *Pop Idol* competition, comes out as gay with no discernible harm to his career (p.35).

1999
Angela Mason (p.73), Executive Director of Stonewall, awarded OBE for services to the lesbian and gay community, and Nick Partridge, Chief Executive of the Terrence Higgins Trust, awarded OBE for services for people affected by HIV and AIDS.

1998
Peter Tatchell (p.98) and three other members of OutRage! seek to make a citizen's arrest of Robert Mugabe for his record on gay rights; Tatchell tries again in Brussels in 2001.

George Michael arrested in Los Angeles for sexual importuning, discusses his sexuality in the media and makes the music video 'Outside', incorporating references to the arrest.

Memorial to Oscar Wilde by lesbian artist Maggi Hambling unveiled in London.

US television network NBC broadcasts *Will & Grace*, the first television series to feature a gay character as one of its main protagonists. The series ran until 2006 and won a total of sixteen Emmy Awards.

2005
Passing of the *Civil Partnerships Act* in UK.

At a lavish ceremony, Elton John and David Furnish are among the first gay people to be publicly partnered in the UK.

2009
Jóhanna Sigurðardóttir becomes Iceland's first female Prime Minister, and the world's first openly gay Premier, on 1 February.

National Portrait Gallery organises an exhibition of gay icons.

▶A CHRONOLOGY OF GAY ICONOGRAPHY

1791
France decriminalises homosexual acts between consenting adults, overturning centuries of Christian tradition.

1796
Bavarian Alois Senefelder invents lithography.

1810
Two schoolteachers in Edinburgh, Jane Pirie and Marianne Woods, are accused by one of their pupils of being a lesbian couple and taken to court; the verdict is 'unproven'.

1826
Frenchman Nicéphore Niépce produces the first photograph.

1867
Karl-Heinrich Ulrichs, openly homosexual, urges a repeal of anti-homosexual laws to the Congress of German Jurists in Munich.

1869
Hungarian Karl-Maria Kertbeny coins the term 'homosexual' in a pamphlet on Paragraph 143 of the Prussian Penal Code.

1946
Foundation of the gay rights organisation COC (Centre for Culture and Recreation) in Amsterdam.

1933
Gertrude Stein publishes The Autobiography of Alice B. Toklas.

1928
Publication of The Well of Loneliness and subsequent trial of Radclyffe Hall (p.14).

1918
Dancer Maud Allan files a libel suit against journalist Noel Pemberton Billing who, in an article entitled 'The Cult of the Clitoris', suggested her lesbianism.

1897
Magnus Hirschfeld, Max Spohr, Eduard Oberg and Max von Bülow found in Berlin the (mainly gay) rights organisation, the Scientific Humanitarian Committee.

1882
Oscar Wilde has his photo taken by Napoleon Sarony in New York prior to his US tour (p.12).

1978
Assassination of openly gay city supervisor Harvey Milk in San Francisco (p.74).

1983
Britain's first openly gay MP Chris Smith elected to parliament. In 1997 he becomes Secretary of State for Culture, Media and Sport (p.77).

1984
Simon Nkoli founds the Saturday Group, South Africa's first black gay organisation. In 1994 he meets with President Nelson Mandela.

1986
First appearance of openly gay character Colin in popular soap opera EastEnders, played by gay actor, Michael Cashman.

The Communards, featuring gay Jimmy Somerville and lesbian-friendly Sarah-Jane Morris, have the UK's highest selling single of the year with 'Don't Leave Me This Way'. It also makes the US Top 40.

1987
Foundation of militant AIDS organisation ACT UP in New York.

1997
In an interview with the Observer, MP Angela Eagle comes out as a lesbian.

Elton John (p.45) sings at the funeral of Diana, Princess of Wales (p.34).

Ellen DeGeneres comes out, to no one's surprise, on her television show Ellen (p.87).

1993
Rock singer Melissa Etheridge comes out at a celebration of Bill Clinton's inauguration as President of the United States.

Country singer k.d. lang (p.94) appears on the cover of Vanity Fair with model Cindy Crawford.

1990
Ian McKellen, already openly gay, is knighted (p.69).

Footballer Justin Fashanu comes out as gay in the Sun newspaper; his career founders and, in 1998, he commits suicide.

Foundation of militant gay activist group OutRage! in the UK.

1989
Foundation of British lesbian, gay and bisexual rights lobby group Stonewall.

1988
Section 28 of the Local Government Act 1988 is passed, prohibiting local authorities, and thus schools, from 'promoting homosexuality or ... the teaching of the acceptability of homosexuality as

a pretended family relationship'. Repealed in Scotland in 2000 and in the rest of the UK in 2003.

THE SELECTORS AND THEIR ICONS

WAHEED ALLI VILLAGE PEOPLE / JEFF STRYKER / LILY SAVAGE / DAVID HOCKNEY / DIANA PRINCESS OF WALES / WILL YOUNG **ALAN HOLLINGHURST** JOE DALLESANDRO / RONALD FIRBANK / GERARD MANLEY HOPKINS / EDMUND WHITE / PYOTR ILYICH TCHAIKOVSKY / THOM GUNN **ELTON JOHN** GIANNI VERSACE / JOHN LENNON / MSTISLAV ROSTROPOVICH / BERNIE TAUPIN / GRAHAM TAYLOR / WINIFRED ATWELL **JACKIE KAY** QUENTIN CRISP / AUDRE LORDE / EDWIN MORGAN / BESSIE SMITH / BILLY TIPTON / SOJOURNER TRUTH **BILLIE JEAN KING** THE MOFFITT FAMILY / ILANA KLOSS / CHRISTIANE AMANPOUR / ALTHEA GIBSON / NELSON MANDELA / BOB RICHARDS **IAN MCKELLEN** MARGARETHE CAMMERMEYER / EDWARD CARPENTER / REGINA FONG / ANGELA MASON / HARVEY MILK / WALT WHITMAN **CHRIS SMITH** EDWIN CAMERON / W.H. AUDEN / BENJAMIN BRITTEN / JOHN MENLOVE EDWARDS / VIRGINIA WOOLF / ALAN TURING **BEN SUMMERSKILL** MAYA ANGELOU / ELLEN DEGENERES / FRANCIS BACON / MARTINA NAVRATILOVA / JOE ORTON / IAN ROBERTS **SANDI TOKSVIG** K.D. LANG / HILDA MATHESON / JANE CHOLMELEY / ROSA BONHEUR / PETER TATCHELL / GENE ROBINSON **SARAH WATERS** DENTON WELCH / PATRICIA HIGHSMITH / BRYHER / DAPHNE DU MAURIER / SYLVIA TOWNSEND WARNER / KENNETH WILLIAMS

Waheed Alli Born in 1964, Lord Waheed Alli was brought up in south London and left school after his O levels. He started work as a junior researcher for the financial magazine *Planned Savings*, where he worked his way up through the organisation. In 1984, the investment group Save & Prosper recruited him as their research director and Alli began his second very successful career in the City, before returning to the magazine as publisher three years later. In the 1990s he made a shift in careers, which gave him both public prominence and commercial success: pairing up with his partner Charlie Parsons and singer Bob Geldof, he formed Planet 24, one of the largest independent production companies in the UK. Alli's media and political connections made him a key behind-the-scenes player in the 1997 election of New Labour and in 1998 he was given a place in the House of Lords, from where he remains an active proponent of Gay Rights and Equality. Today Alli is Executive Chairman of the media rights company Chorion, Chairman of Asos, one of the UK's largest online fashion retailers, and Director of Olga Productions, which produces *The Paul O'Grady Show*. He is also a trustee of the Elton John AIDS Foundation, Chancellor of De Montfort University, Leicester, President of the National Youth Theatre and a patron of a number of other voluntary organisations.

Lord Waheed Alli
Mary McCartney, 2008
National Portrait Gallery, London
© Mary McCartney

Village People
(Formed 1977)

It is hard to look at the line-up of the Village People without thinking: GAY. After visiting a fancy-dress night at the gay disco Les Mouches in New York's Greenwich Village, French music producer Jacques Morali was inspired to create the popular disco band which went on to produce hits such as 'In the Navy' and 'YMCA'. The stereotype costumes of cowboys, bikers, construction workers and police officers were coupled with an overtly camp musical style, so that the Village People came to represent an iconic caricature of gay life in the 1980s.

Village People
CBS Photo Archive, 1977
Courtesy of Getty Images

Jeff Stryker
Pierre et Gilles, 1991
Courtesy Galerie Jérôme
de Noirmont
© Pierre et Gilles

Jeff Stryker
(b.1962)

There is no question that the act of sex has been, and always will be, a defining aspect to sexuality. As a gay porn star, Jeff Stryker is immediately recognisable among gay men as the literal embodiment of this side to sexuality. But Stryker's iconic status is derived from something larger than just acting: it is his unashamed commercialisation, from 'Stryker Lube' and the 'Jeff Stryker Action Figure' to the best-selling 'Jeff Stryker Cock and Balls', a dildo cast directly from his erect penis. By capitalising on his celebrity status in this way, he ensured that he was the first gay porn star to become a brand in his own right.

Lily Savage
Paul Massey, 2003
Camera Press, London

Lily Savage, Paul O'Grady's drag alter ego, began her life on the gay bar and club circuit of the 1970s and 1980s. Her personality, though, reflects working-class values and humour as much as it reveals the eclectic background from which she originates. After a hit performance at the Edinburgh Festival, she broke out into national popular television and has since endured as one of the most recognisable characters in British comedy. Lily Savage is not just a gay icon; she is also an icon of the mainstream, and an icon of the working class.

Lily Savage
(b.1955)

David Hockney
Peter Macdiarmid, 2005
Courtesy of Getty Images

David Hockney
(b.1937)

The expression of homosexuality in David Hockney's work is at once cautious and confident. While frequently using his artistic talent to elevate and broadcast the sexualised male figure to a wide cultural audience, the approach is often voyeuristic, reminding us that these are not simply 'images' but rather subjects which have some sort of relationship with the viewer. In reminding us of this relationship, Hockney directs attention back to himself and his own sexuality. His striking images therefore explore the conflict between the public and the private spheres, which will always be far more a concern of gay life than they are of straight life.

Princess Diana continues to live on as an icon for many different people in many different ways: fashion icon, charity icon, feminist icon, British icon. Her place as a gay icon, however, was cemented by a single moment during a visit to a 'Chain of Hope' centre in April 1987. Taking the hand of an AIDS victim she shattered the widely held belief that physical contact alone could lead to the contraction of AIDS, and offered hope and comfort to those in the gay community infected with the HIV virus. The photograph of this gesture became an enduring icon of compassion and understanding in the face of ostracism and suspicion, the spirit of which, along with her sense of style and natural beauty, is also reflected in Terence Donovan's portrait of Diana.

Diana, Princess of Wales
(1961–97)

Diana, Princess of Wales
Terence Donovan, 1986
National Portrait Gallery,
London (NPG P716(1))

Will Young
Alan Olley, 2003
Camera Press, London

Will Young
(b.1979)

When Will Young achieved a come-from-behind victory in the first ever *Pop Idol* contest of 2002, it showed that Britain was changing. Although not openly gay at the time, Young revealed his sexuality a month after winning the competition and became an instant gay icon thereafter. Through a telephone vote open to the public, in which nearly nine million people participated, his success came neither because of, nor in spite of, his sexuality. By not allowing his sexuality to define his music he became a role model to the gay community, and also to an entire generation of new young talent. Since 2002 the *Pop Idol* format has been exported around the world, and Young's continued success as a viable artist has made him an inspiration for countless others in the years since.

Alan Hollinghurst
Mary McCartney, 2008
National Portrait Gallery, London
© Mary McCartney

Alan Hollinghurst   Born in Stroud in Gloucestershire, England, in 1954, Alan Hollinghurst was educated at Magdalen College, Oxford. He was on the staff of the *Times Literary Supplement* from 1982 to 1995. He is the author of four novels that explore gay experience over the past century: *The Swimming-Pool Library* (1988), which won a Somerset Maugham Award, *The Folding Star* (1994), which won the James Tait Black Memorial Prize (for fiction), *The Spell* (1998) and *The Line of Beauty* (2004), which won the Man Booker Prize and was adapted by Andrew Davies for BBC Television.

Joe Dallesandro
(b.1948)

Joe Dallesandro worked as a model and hustler before being discovered by the icon-maker Andy Warhol, who gave him a starring role in classic underground movies such as *Flesh* (1968), *Trash* (1970) and *Heat* (1972), all directed by Paul Morrissey. Dallesandro's sexy physique, expressionless beauty and modest acting skills were perfect for the deadpan, voyeuristic Warhol style, and he became the most widely recognised of the Warhol instant 'superstars' of the 1970s, a supremely ambivalent sex symbol. As Warhol himself said, 'In my movies, everyone's in love with Joe Dallesandro.'

Joe Dallesandro
Paul Morrissey, 1968
Private Collection

Ronald Firbank
Bertram Park, 1917
Camera Press, London

Ronald Firbank
(1886–1926)

Ronald Firbank (born Arthur Annesley Ronald Firbank) was one of the most original English novelists of the twentieth century. In books such as *Caprice* (1917), *Valmouth* (1919) and *The Flower beneath the Foot* (1923) he threw out all the baggage of the Victorian novel, and with it most of Victorian morality. Shy, dandyish, heavy-drinking, Firbank led the life of a solitary nomad, writing in hotels and rented apartments in southern Europe, North Africa and the Caribbean. His slender fictions, made out of glittering fragments of talk and description, reflect his eccentric wit as well as his pervasive melancholy. He is celebrated as a master of high camp, but he was also a radical technician and radical homosexualiser of the novel.

Gerard Manley Hopkins
Hills & Saunders, probably
by George Giberne, 1863
National Portrait Gallery,
London (NPG P452)

Gerard Manley Hopkins
(1844–89)

The extreme originality of Gerald Manley Hopkins's poetry
flourished in conditions of near total secrecy. He was a
Jesuit priest, living under the exacting dictates of his order,
and his poems, seen in manuscript by a mere handful of
trusted friends, were not published until twenty-nine years
after his death. In his work, his love and admiration for other
men finds natural and exuberant expression as a part of
his love for God. Hopkins is one of the great innovators
in English poetry, not only in the verse technique he called
sprung rhythm, but in the unabashed disclosure of his
given sexuality.

Edmund White

(b.1940)

Edmund White is often referred to as a chronicler of the epochs in gay history that he has lived through: the anxieties and confusions of life before liberation; the Stonewall moment; the sexual free-for-all that followed; and the terrible crisis of AIDS. But his groundbreaking novels, such as *A Boy's Own Story* (1982) and *The Farewell Symphony* (1997), do more than this: they see gay history, his own and others', through the lens of an extraordinary imagination, lyrical but unsparing, observant but obsessive. White made contemporary gay fiction possible, and remains its greatest exponent.

Edmund White
Marion Ettlinger, 2000
© Marion Ettlinger

Pyotr Ilyich Tchaikovsky
Unknown photographer, 1890
Courtesy of Getty Images

Pyotr Ilyich Tchaikovsky

(1840–93)

Tchaikovsky's astounding melodic gifts, his intensely subjective lyricism, his gripping portrayal in music of the beauty of life menaced by inexorable fate – all these things have kept him among the most popular of composers. He is also the first great composer whose personality and life were self-evidently and testifiably gay. Awareness of this fact over the past century has fed a certain strain of homophobic distaste for the emotionalism and supposed 'hysteria' of works like the *Symphonie Pathétique* – works in which we now celebrate the fusion of highly personal insight with unanswerable musical form.

At the age of twenty-five, Thom (Thomson William) Gunn left England to join his lover Mike Kitay in California, and remained there for the rest of his life. Gayness was the trigger for his escape, an integral element of his art and of his glamour. He was a poet steeped in English poetry of the Renaissance who also wrote in exploratory free verse about drug experience and the sexual freedoms of his adopted San Francisco. A superb verse technician, he was also the pre-eminent explorer, celebrator and, through the AIDS years, elegist of the gay culture he so fully and vigilantly inhabited.

Thom Gunn
(1929–2004)

Elton John Born Reginald Kenneth Dwight in Middlesex, England, in 1947, Sir Elton John's music career has spanned four decades. He has sold more than 200 million records, making him one of the most successful musicians of all time. John studied at the Royal Academy of Music in London and formed his first band Bluesology in 1964. Between 1970 and 1976, with producer Gus Dudgeon and lyricist Bernie Taupin, he made an astonishing fourteen albums. He was honoured with the Best British Male Artist Brit Award in 1991, inducted into the Rock and Roll Hall of Fame in 1994, won five Grammy awards between 1986 and 2000 and the Grammy Legend Award in 2001. John first came out as being bisexual in 1976, and later came out as being gay. Horrified and angered at the magnitude of HIV/AIDS and what little was being done, he set up the Elton John AIDS Foundation in 1992. In 1998 John was honoured with a knighthood for services to music and charitable services. Since its inception, the Foundation has given out more than £50,000,000 of funding for HIV/AIDS projects in fifty-five countries across the world.

Gianni Versace
Andy Warhol, 1980
The Andy Warhol Museum,
Pittsburgh; Contribution
The Andy Warhol Foundation
for the Visual Arts, Inc.

Gianni Versace
(1946–97)

Undoubtedly one of the most talented fashion designers of the twentieth century, Gianni Versace's inspiration came from art everywhere – Ancient Greek and Roman, pop and contemporary – he had such eclectic and exquisite taste. Versace was my mentor: it was through his guidance and the time spent with him at his various houses that I developed my love of art and photography. In terms of fashion, Versace's heyday was the era of the supermodels; everything about his style was perfect for that time. He was a dear, dear friend and a phenomenal man.

John Lennon

(1940–80)

John Lennon is the second of my icons
(like Gianni Versace) to have had their
lives foreshortened by a gunman.
There is no disputing John's talents as
a musician or a songwriter, either with
the Beatles or in his solo career. Yet to
me there is always the sadness of not
knowing what might have been when he
seemed to be reaching another creative
peak. In the 1960s his songwriting was
a huge inspiration to me and in the
1970s we both had solo careers,
became friends, and enjoyed a US
number one single with our 1974 duet
'Whatever Gets You Thru the Night'.
I had a bet with John that the track
would be a number one hit. Losing the
bet, he agreed to perform on stage
with me at Madison Square Garden,
New York. In addition to the single
we performed 'Lucy in the Sky with
Diamonds' and 'I Saw Her Standing
There'. That happened to be the last live
concert Lennon would ever play and
it became a defining moment for me.

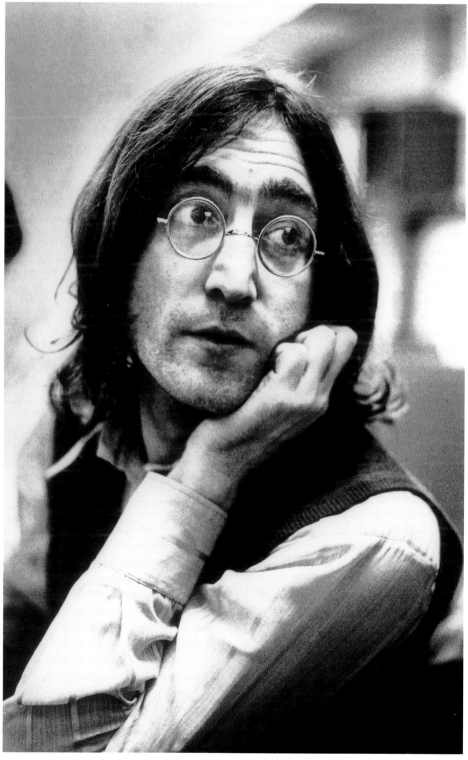

John Lennon
Linda McCartney, 1968
National Portrait Gallery,
London (NPG P575)

Mstislav Rostropovich
(1927–2007)

Mstislav Leopoldovich Rostropovich, or Slava as he is known affectionately, was without doubt for me the greatest cellist ever. Composers including Sergei Prokofiev, Dmitri Shostakovich and Leonard Bernstein all wrote pieces specifically for him. Beyond the music, Rostropovich fought for freedom of speech, artistic freedom and was an early supporter of dissidents such as Aleksandr Solzhenitsyn. Before long, he faced no option but to leave the USSR and to settle in the USA in 1974. There he continued to champion human rights, funded international social and cultural projects and supported young musicians, while conducting and directing some leading orchestras, and, in 1983, founded the Rostropovich Festival. He was a charming man and a completely inspirational force.

Mstislav Rostropovich
Lord Snowdon, 1991
Camera Press, London

Bernie Taupin
(b.1950)

Bernie Taupin has been my lyricist and writing partner since 1969. I have always admired Bernie so much – the Lincolnshire-born, 'Wild West'-loving boy, who went to London to seek fame and fortune, created the character of the 'Brown Dirt Cowboy' (for the *Captain Fantastic* album) and went on to live the very life he craved by moving to southern California in 1970, where he now owns a ranch and cutting horses. As we mark our forty-year writing partnership, Bernie is no mere 'collaborator' – beyond his 2006 Golden Globe Award for *Brokeback Mountain*, his hits with other musical artists such as Heart and Starship, and his books of poems – he is without doubt an icon for me.

Bernie Taupin
Terry O'Neill, 1975
Courtesy of
the photographer

Graham Taylor
(b.1944)

Graham Taylor was a good footballer but a truly great manager, famed for his love of the 'long ball' style game, getting the ball fast and direct to the forwards. In 1977 Graham came on board to manage my then newly purchased football club – Watford. He even turned down a job offer from West Bromwich Albion (then in the First Division) to manage Watford – a club in the Fourth Division. I had been a lifelong Watford fan and Graham truly made whatever dreams I had for my team come true. In only five seasons Graham took Watford from the Fourth Division to the First, and of course to the FA Cup final in 1984. After going on to manage the England team, he came back to Watford in 1996 and again the team's fortunes went up – this time to the Premier League.

Graham Taylor
Mark Lawrence, 1992
Mark Lawrence/Rex Features

Winifred Atwell

(1914–83)

Born in Trinidad, Winifred Atwell was one of the most popular piano players and, indeed, instrumentalists of the 1950s and 1960s. She was a pioneer – from being the first woman to receive the highest grading at London's Royal Academy of Music to topping the bill at the London Palladium. Her musicianship was exemplary, and her 'honky-tonk' style groundbreaking and amazing, with a repertoire extending from classic reinterpretations of Gershwin through to 'Roll Out the Barrel'. She loved touring and playing live, and was the total 'showman'. Winifred Atwell's piano performances were simply captivating. She showed me what was possible and was a total inspiration.

Winifred Atwell
Unknown photographer, 1950s
Courtesy of Getty Images

Jackie Kay Born in 1961, Jackie Kay was brought up in Scotland. Her most recent collection of short stories, *Wish I Was Here* (2006), won the British Book Awards Decibel Writer of the Year. She has won the Guardian Fiction Prize for her novel *Trumpet* (1998), and a Forward Poetry Prize for her collection of poetry *The Adoption Papers* (1991). She is Professor of Creative Writing at the University of Newcastle. Her most recent collection of poetry *Darling: New and Selected Poems* (2007) was a Poetry Book Society Recommendation. She was awarded an MBE for services to literature in 2006. Her most recent collection for children, *Red, Cherry Red* (2007) won the CLPE Poetry Award. *The Lamplighter*, her long poem to commemorate the abolition of the slave trade, was published in September 2008. She lives in Manchester with her son.

Jackie Kay
Mary McCartney, 2008
National Portrait Gallery, London
© Mary McCartney

Quentin Crisp
(1908–99)

Quentin Crisp was born Dennis Charles Pratt on Christmas Day 1908. He died in Manchester in 1999. Right up until his death Quentin remained resolutely and independently himself, amusing people with his memorable and insightful witticisms, his grandeur and intelligence. He is most well known for his book about his life, the classic *The Naked Civil Servant* (1968), which charts his own bravery, his refusal to stay in the closet. Quentin was out long before others, and Quentin was queenly long before 'queens' came in, and Quentin was gay before the gay days. He was often beaten for dressing up but they never battered his inimitable spirit, which inspired John Hurt's famous portrayal in the television version of *The Naked Civil Servant* in 1975. Sting dedicated his song 'Englishman in New York' to Quentin and he was also chronicled in Andy Warhol's diaries.

Quentin Crisp
Fergus Greer, 1989
National Portrait Gallery
London (NPG x126805)

Audre Lorde
(1934–92)

Poet, mother, lesbian, feminist, Caribbean-American, Audre Lorde believed in naming the names, convinced that silence is the greatest enemy. *Zami: A New Spelling of My Name* (1983) was a brave book that addressed the particular complexities of being a black lesbian. She wrote courageously about breast cancer in *The Cancer Journals* (1980). She refused to have a prosthesis after her mastectomy, and then, in admirable Lorde style, made a fashion out of being asymmetrical – wearing one long earring and one stud! She was a modern-day woman warrior, an admirer of the Dahomean Amazons – she wrote about them in her most unified collection of poetry *The Black Unicorn* (1978). In the final years of her life she lived in the Virgin Islands with her partner Gloria Joseph. For many people Lorde's voice was a voice in the wilderness.

Audre Lorde
Colleen McKay, c1980s
Courtesy the photographer

Edwin Morgan
Colin Mearns, 2008
Courtesy of the Herald
Picture Archive, Glasgow

Edwin Morgan
(b.1920)

Edwin Morgan is one of the foremost Scottish poets of the twentieth century, and his work has been a huge influence on younger poets. There is nothing Morgan won't write about – Glasgow, love, computers, science, midges, strawberries, the Loch Ness Monster – his poetry is witty, incisive and incredibly various. In 1982 he was awarded an OBE and in 2004 he was named the first Scottish National Poet, the Scots Makar. He wrote a poem especially for the opening of the Scottish Parliament in 2004. Morgan came out as a gay man in 1990 partly in response to Clause 28. I visited him recently in his old people's home and marvelled at the lack of clutter in his room, at the presence simply of books, foreign dictionaries and paintings. He is a brilliant translator and in his old age he also seems skilled at translating one experience into another.

Bessie Smith
(1894–1937)

Bessie Smith was the most popular blues singer of the 1920s and early 1930s, and at that time was the highest-paid black woman in America. She was nicknamed the Empress of the Blues, and her particular style of singing was to influence generations of jazz singers. A few days after Smith recorded her last song, Billie Holiday went into the same studio to record her first. A feisty woman who liked her moonshine and her pigs' feet, Smith always stood up for herself. She sang in blues tents to thousands of people. But when blues went out and jazz came in, Bessie Smith's fortunes fell and her signature tune, 'Nobody Knows You When You're Down and Out', began to seem prescient. She was bisexual and practically an alcoholic – the perfect icon! After she died – in a controversial car crash – 7,000 people attended her funeral.

Bessie Smith
Unknown photographer, c.1920s
Courtesy of Getty Images

Billy Tipton (centre)
Unknown photographer, 1951
© Private Collection

Billy Tipton
(1914–89)

Billy Lee Tipton (born Dorothy Lucille Tipton) was an American jazz pianist and saxophonist. He became the subject of public interest posthumously when it was revealed that Tipton, who had lived for decades as a man, was biologically female. This story inspired me to write my novel *Trumpet*. I came across a short article in a newspaper, which quoted one of Tipton's adopted sons as saying, 'He'll always be Daddy to me,' and I found that profoundly moving. It made me think love is a matter of belief: if you love someone enough, you'll believe them. Identity is fluid, not fixed. Tipton's life inspired Diane Middlebrook to write the biography *Suits Me: The Double Life of Billy Tipton* (1998). Some female jazz musicians formed the Billy Tipton Memorial Saxophone Quartet shortly after his death.

Sojourner Truth
Unknown photographer, 1864
Courtesy of the Library of Congress,
Washington, DC

Sojourner Truth
(1797–1883)

Sojourner Truth was the self-given name of Isabella Baumfree who was born into slavery in Swartekill, New York. She was an abolitionist and is best known for her famous speech 'Ain't I a Woman?', which she delivered to the Ohio Women's Rights Convention in 1851: 'That man over there says that women need to be helped into carriages, and lifted over ditches, and to have the best place everywhere. Nobody ever helps me into carriages, or over mud-puddles, or gives me any best place! And ain't I a woman? Look at me! Look at my arm! I have ploughed and planted, and gathered into barns, and no man could head me! And ain't I a woman? I could work as much and eat as much as a man – when I could get it – and bear the lash as well! And ain't I a woman? I have borne five children, and seen most all sold off to slavery, and when I cried out with my mother's grief, none but Jesus heard me! And ain't I a woman?'

Billie Jean King
Mary McCartney, 2008
National Portrait Gallery, London
© Mary McCartney

Billie Jean King

Born in Long Beach, California, in 1943, Billie Jean King won her first tennis championship when she was just fourteen years old. She went on to win thirty-nine Grand Slam singles, doubles and mixed double titles including twenty at Wimbledon over a career spanning two decades. A champion for the women's movement, she challenged the Establishment and drew attention to the inequality in prize money afforded to women's champions compared to men. King is best known for her triumph over tennis-pro Bobby Riggs, who had said that no woman could ever beat him, in the 'Battle of the Sexes' tennis match in 1973. She was the first American athlete to acknowledge having a homosexual relationship. King retired from professional play in 1984 and now serves on the boards of the Women's Sports Foundation as well as the Elton John AIDS Foundation. In 1995 King joined the Virginia Slims Legends tour to raise money and awareness for the fight against HIV/AIDS. She also launched GreenSlam in 2007, an environmental initiative that issued a challenge to the sports industry to become more proactive about 'going green'.

My family shaped and guided me to be the person I am today. We grew up in a middle-class home in Long Beach, California, where my father was a firefighter and my mother was a homemaker who sold Avon and Tupperware so my brother and I could pursue our dreams. For more than a decade my brother Randy was a major league baseball relief pitcher, mostly with the San Francisco Giants. My family gave me unconditional love, was my moral compass and taught me the importance of respecting others.

Bill, Betty and Randy Moffitt

Ilana Kloss

(b.1956)

Ilana Kloss is the love of my life. We are partners in business and in life. An accomplished athlete, Ilana was the number one doubles player in the world in 1976 and the youngest player ever to reach number one in her native South Africa. Prior to turning professional she won both the Wimbledon and US Open Junior titles. Today she is the CEO and Commissioner of World TeamTennis, the co-ed tennis format founded in 1974, serves on the board of the Elton John AIDS Foundation and is a past chair of the Women's Sports Foundation. Ilana leads by example and shares without hesitation.

Ilana Kloss
Unknown photographer, 2009
Courtesy of Getty Images

Bill, Betty and Randy Moffitt
Photographer unknown, c.1970s
Private Collection

Christiane Amanpour
(b.1958)

The daughter of an Iranian father and
a British mother, Christiane Amanpour is
the epitome of global achievement.
As one of the world's leading journalists
she has reported on all the major crises
from the world's many hot spots.
Amanpour's understanding of the
importance of history and her unique
ability to secure interviews with prominent
figures have allowed her to cover
some of the world's most important
stories. Yet it is Amanpour's deep
commitment to friendship and her
delightful conversational nature that
highlight the best parts of her soul.

Christiane Amanpour
Brent Stirton, 2007
© Brent Stirton/Getty Images for CNN

Althea Gibson
(1927–2003)

The first woman of colour ever to win a major tennis title, Althea Gibson was breaking down barriers long before the birth of women's professional tennis as we know it today. Gibson captured the attention of the world with her win at the 1956 French Championships and went on to add four other major titles, including the 1957 and 1958 titles at both Wimbledon and the US Championships. She competed at a time when the players received no money and her home country was segregated, yet Gibson lived her life as a champion, opening doors for those who would follow her and always entertaining and enlightening those around her.

Althea Gibson
Reg Birkett/Douglas Miller, 1958
Courtesy of Getty Images

Nelson Mandela
(b.1918)

Nelson Mandela changed our world. One man. One heart. One mind. I hope to meet him some day and, when I do, I know I will learn from his wisdom and I will promise to carry his message forward. He has touched my heart, just as he has influenced the hearts and minds of people all over the world. He freed South Africa and put a constitution and government in place that stands today as one of the true examples of democracy. We need to learn from his spirit and we must remain committed to ensuring his legacy lives for all time.

Nelson Mandela
Ian Berry, 1994
Ian Berry/Magnum Photos

Bob Richards
(b.1926)

The Reverend Bob Richards won two Olympic gold medals and was the first athlete to appear on a Wheaties box. However, it was his calling as a minister that moved me. From the time I was eleven until I turned fourteen the Reverend Richards was our pastor at the First Church of the Brethren in Long Beach, California. Reverend Richards inspired me. He had a wonderful ability to work sports metaphors into his sermons and that not only challenged me, but taught me the importance of being true to yourself. He helped me to understand that it was not enough to have a dream, you had to allow yourself to live the dream.

Reverend Bob Richards
Unknown photographer, 1952
IOC Olympic Museum Collections

Ian McKellen Born in 1939 in Lancashire, England, Sir Ian McKellen has acted onstage in classical and new plays since his schooldays at Bolton School in north-west England. His stage roles have been many and varied – most recently as King Lear for the Royal Shakespeare Company's world tour and next as Gogo in *Waiting for Godot*. On screen he has played Richard III, Gandalf, Magneto and the gay film director James Whale in *Gods and Monsters* (1998), for which he received an Academy Award nomination as Best Actor. Since coming out twenty years ago, he has argued for the rights of gay people in the UK. In 1989 he was a co-founder of Stonewall UK, the lesbian, gay and bisexual rights lobby group, and is patron of a number of groups for gay people and their friends and families. In 2008 he was appointed a Companion of Honour for services to drama and to equality.

Margarethe Cammermeyer
Andreea Dragomir, 2008
Grethe Cammermeyer

Margarethe Cammermeyer
(b.1942)

Margarethe Cammermeyer is a former colonel in the Washington National Guard and a gay-rights activist. She loved the US army and served on active duty in the USA, Germany and Vietnam. After disclosing she was lesbian in 1989, she was honourably discharged from the military on 11 June 1992. Cammermeyer filed a lawsuit against the decision in civil court and in June 1994 a judge ruled that both her discharge, and the ban on gays and lesbians serving in the military, was unconstitutional. Cammermeyer returned to the National Guard and served as one of the few officially accepted openly gay or lesbian people in the military up until her retirement in 1997. Since then, she has campaigned against the US military's 'don't ask, don't tell' policy, has run unsuccessfully for Congress and has also published *Serving in Silence* (1994), her autobiography that was made into a television film starring Glenn Close. In 1995 on the March on Washington dc, she spoke with determination and passion: 'Find a place where you are appreciated for all of you – serve that organisation for the greater good.' Her example is unmatched.

Edward Carpenter
(1844–1929)

A philosopher and poet, Edward Carpenter inspired the early socialists and advocated causes that were not to become popular until recently. Open about his sexuality, Carpenter was crucial to the eventual development of the gay liberation movement. In his foundational text *The Intermediate Sex: A Study of Some Transitional Types of Men and Women* (1908) he wrote: 'The Uranian [these days 'gay'] people may be destined to form the advance guard of that great movement which will one day transform the common life, by substituting the bond of personal affection and compassion for the monetary, legal and other external ties which now control and confine society.' Filled with continued political radicalism, the last two decades of Carpenter's life were characterised by his persistent involvement in progressive issues, such as environmental protection, animal rights, sexual freedom, the Women's Movement and vegetarianism.

Edward Carpenter (detail)
Alfred Mattison, copied by
Emery Walker Ltd, 1905
National Portrait Gallery,
London (NPG x87106)

Regina Fong

(1945–2003)

Reg Bundy trained as a dancer but by 1985 his alter ego Her Imperial Highness Regina Fong had taken over his career, in London gay bars and clubs that welcomed outrageous drag acts. Her Imperial Highness claimed to be a Romanoff but, despite her aristocratic orange hair and far-fetched gowns, was right down to earth with a bossy, biting tongue for hecklers. This was drag for the people, of course mostly gay people, who saw him on Tuesday nights at the Black Cap, or in the confines of the East End's White Swan, where he used to change in a cupboard with a bucket for a loo before his midnight forty-minute show on the tiny pub stage. Alongside Lily Savage (p.32), Adrella, Dave Lynn, the Trollettes and so on, Regina Fong belongs to a time when gay people only felt truly safe in the company of their own kind.

H.I.H. Regina Fong
Unknown photographer, 2003
Private Collection

Angela Mason
(b.1944)

Anyone who follows the campaign for legal equality for gay people in the UK appreciates Angela Mason's hard work and strong leadership as director of Stonewall UK from 1992 to 2002 and since. Politicians in both Government and the Opposition have been educated by her dogged advocacy. All gay people are in her debt for the reform of laws that once blighted their lives and disgraced the nation. She has a civil partnership with fellow activist Elizabeth Wilson, with whom she brought up their daughter Ellie. She was awarded an OBE for services to homosexual rights in 1999. As she soldiers on for equality in local areas she worries: 'We are not going back to the dark ages but I don't feel we have kind of cracked it.' The fight continues.

Angela Mason
Maggie Murray for Format
Photographers, 1999
National Portrait Gallery,
London (NPG x132183)

Harvey Milk was an American politician and in 1977 became the first openly gay man to be elected to public office in the USA. As a city supervisor in San Francisco he believed in the importance of gay visiblity: 'A gay official is needed not only for our protection, but to set an example for younger gays that says that the system works. Gay people, we will not win our rights by staying quietly in our closets.... We are coming out! We are coming out to fight the lies, the myths, the distortions! We are coming out to tell the truth about gays!' Despite his national profile and his popularity with his constituents, he was assassinated by a disgruntled colleague in 1978, a martyrdom which is retold in *Milk* (2008), the film starring Sean Penn.

Harvey Milk
(1930–78)

Walt Whitman
(1819–92)

Walt Whitman's renown as a poet is justly universal, but in his lifetime his work *Leaves of Grass* (1855) was banned and this act seems to have cost him his living as a teacher. He pre-dates modern reform movements and was ambiguous about his sexuality, although Oscar Wilde seemed in no doubt: 'I have the kiss of Walt Whitman still on my lips.' His posthumous iconic status among gay people comes from his verse, where our lives are acknowledged and serenaded, as in his poem 'When I Heard at the Close of the Day' (1900):

'For the one I love most lay sleeping by me under the same cover in the cool night,

In the stillness in the autumn moonbeams his face was inclined toward me,

And his arm lay lightly around my breast – and that night I was happy.'

Chris Smith   The Rt. Hon. Lord Smith of Finsbury was born in Barnet, England, in 1951. Educated at George Watson's College in Edinburgh and Pembroke College, Cambridge, he gained a First Class Honours degree in English and a Ph.D. with a thesis on Coleridge and Wordsworth. After working for a housing charity he became a councillor in the London Borough of Islington before winning the Islington South and Finsbury seat at the 1983 general election. A Labour MP from 1983 to 2005, he was Secretary of State for Culture, Media and Sport from 1997 to 2001. Smith co-authored *Suicide of the West* (2006) and is currently Chairman of the Environment Agency and Chairman of the Advertising Standards Authority, Chairman of the Wordsworth Trust and the Donmar Warehouse Theatre, Honorary Fellow of Pembroke College, Cambridge, and Visiting Professor at the University of the Arts London. Smith was Britain's first openly gay MP. In 2006 he entered into a civil partnership with his long-time partner Dorian Jabri.

Lord Chris Smith
Mary McCartney, 2008
National Portrait Gallery, London
© Mary McCartney

Edwin Cameron
(b.1953)

South African Edwin Cameron was a
Rhodes Scholar and became a leading
human rights lawyer in 1986. President
Nelson Mandela appointed him an
Acting Judge of the High Court to chair
a commission into illegal arms deals
in October 1994. He was appointed
permanently to the High Court in 1995
and is now a Judge on the Supreme
Court of South Africa. Cameron was
the first senior South African official to
say publicly not only that he is gay, but
that he is living with HIV. In a country
with over five million people who have
HIV, Cameron's brave stand has helped
to counter prejudice and to transform
attitudes to the epidemic.

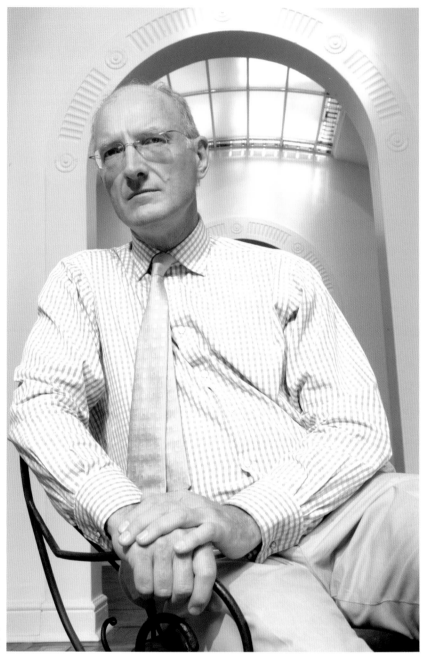

Edwin Cameron
Piers Allardyce, 2005
Courtesy the photographer

W.H. Auden
(1907–73)

One of the greatest poets of the twentieth century, W.H. Auden has left us with a remarkable body of work, both written alone and in collaboration with his lifelong friend Christopher Isherwood. Auden's life took him from the hedonism of Berlin to ambulance driving during the Spanish Civil War to teaching in America to the Professorship of Poetry at Oxford in 1955. One of the commanding literary figures of modern times, and forthrightly gay, Auden was a poet whose work is imbued with a sense of the connectedness of human beings.

W.H. Auden
Cecil Beaton, 1967
National Portrait Gallery,
London (NPG x40007)

Benjamin Britten

(1913–76)

Probably the greatest of all British composers, Benjamin Britten's œuvre includes a vast array of operas, songs, orchestral and choral works, and a formidable *War Requiem*, as well as one of the most important and enduring music festivals of the world, at Aldeburgh in Suffolk, England. The lifelong lover, friend and colleague of the singer Peter Pears, Britten wove the tension brought by his own sexuality (and by his pacifism) into his work. His gayness deepened his music, and his legacy is all the stronger for it.

Benjamin Britten, Baron Britten
Cecil Beaton, 1942
National Portrait Gallery,
London (NPG x14036)

John Menlove Edwards

(1910–58)

One of the leading British rock climbers
and mountaineers of the inter-war years,
John Menlove Edwards made a series
of classic first ascents in Snowdonia in
North Wales, wrote with passion – in
prose and poetry – about his climbing
and about the mountains, was a brilliant
psychiatrist and was a conscientious
objector during the Second World War.
Menlove was gay, and a Christian, and
argued always for mutual acceptance
and understanding in society. His sense
of isolation and the lack of acceptance
by others, however, led him to commit
suicide at the age of forty-seven.

John Menlove Edwards
Geoffrey Bartrum, c.1930s
Private Collection

Virginia Woolf
(1882–1941)

Virginia Woolf's literary achievements were huge. Her novels were among the very best of the early twentieth century, written in an innovative and psychologically astute style. *To the Lighthouse* (1927) and *The Waves* (1931) must rank high on anyone's list of the great English novels. One of the commanding figures of the Bloomsbury Group, who famously 'lived in squares, painted in circles and loved in triangles', Virginia Woolf was married to Leonard Woolf but had a long and emotional affair over many years with Vita Sackville-West.

Virginia Woolf (detail)
Gisèle Freund, 1939
National Portrait Gallery,
London (NPG P440)

Alan Turing
Elliott and Fry, 1951
National Portrait Gallery,
London (NPG x82217)

Alan Turing
(1912–54)

Mathematician, code-breaker, philosopher, inventor of the computer, Alan Mathison Turing was one of the most brilliant men of the first half of the twentieth century, but the refusal of post-war society to accept his sexuality – indeed the attempt to force him to renounce it – drove him to commit suicide at the age of forty-one. Without Turing the Enigma codes of the Second World War would not have been broken. Without Turing computer science would have been far longer coming of age. Yet it is to our eternal shame as a nation that – far from honouring him – we drove him to his death. We can and should honour him now.

Ben Summerskill Born in 1961 in Kent, Ben Summerskill studied at Merton College, Oxford, and was appointed the Chief Executive of the UK-based lesbian, gay and bisexual rights lobby organisation Stonewall in 2003, now the largest gay equality body in Europe. He led parliamentary campaigns for the introduction of civil partnership and also for pioneering new protections for gay people against discrimination in the delivery of public services, introduced in 2007. At Stonewall he has led significant growth during which membership of Stonewall's Diversity Champions programme for major employers has risen from thirty-five members to over 400, employing almost five million people between them. In 2005 Stonewall launched an Education for All programme, supported by a coalition of over seventy organisations, to tackle homophobia and homophobic bullying in schools. Until 2003 Summerskill had spent twelve years as a journalist. He was previously Assistant Editor of the *Observer* and has also worked as Media Editor for the *Daily Express* and at the *London Evening Standard*. In December 2006 he was appointed a Commissioner at the new Commission for Equality and Human Rights.

Ben Summerskill
Mary McCartney, 2008
National Portrait Gallery, London
© Mary McCartney

Maya Angelou
(b.1928)

Discovering the work of polymathic poet, author, actress and civil rights activist Maya Angelou was transformative for me. Her autobiographies – from *I Know Why the Caged Bird Sings* (1969) onwards – are a potent reminder that human beings can determinedly aspire to change in the face of prejudice. 'I couldn't tell him about living inside a skin that was hated or feared by the majority of one's fellow citizens,' Angelou wrote in 1976, convinced that: 'It's time for parents to teach young people early on that in diversity there is beauty and there is strength.'

Ellen DeGeneres
Michael Thompson, 2005
Courtesy the photographer

Maya Angelou
Michael Ochs Archive, 1970
Courtesy of Getty Images

Ellen DeGeneres
(b.1958)

She's just so cool. The comedienne, television host and actress came out to the world in 1997, appearing on the cover of *Time* magazine proclaiming: 'Yep, I'm gay.' DeGeneres overcame a fiercely orchestrated backlash from the so-called Christian Right and more recently successfully weathered the storm of religious broadcaster Pat Robinson blaming her personally for Hurricane Katrina. DeGeneres's fitting response to her critics has been her own twenty-five Emmy award-winning prime-time talk show and she's become one of the most successful women on television. A true icon, DeGeneres is an inspiration to millions.

Francis Bacon
(1909–92)

Francis Bacon's dark genius made him one of the greatest artists of the twentieth century, but his appeal for me was that he was also unashamedly gay. His willingness to depict his lovers in his work (and explain exactly who they were) was as compelling to me as a young man as his austere style. The emotional rawness was certainly something with which most people growing up gay in the 1970s could identify. Margaret Thatcher's tart description of him as 'that dreadful man who paints those horrible pictures' did not put me off.

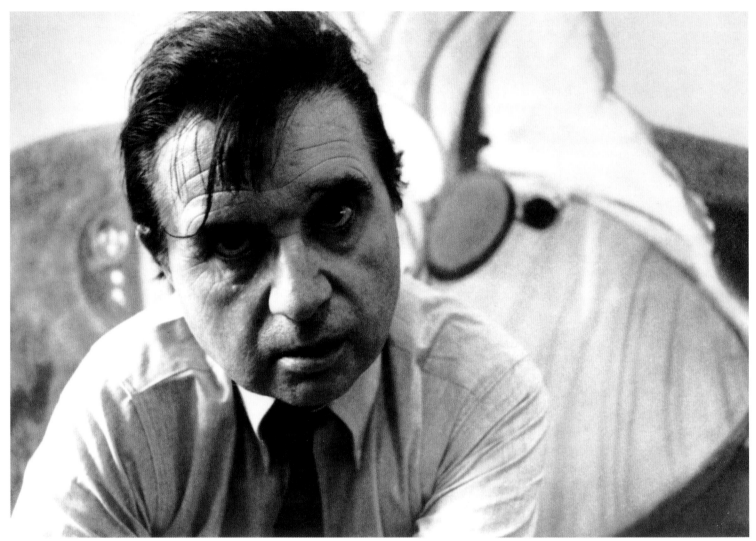

Francis Bacon
John Hedgecoe, 1970
National Portrait Gallery,
London (NPG P158)

Martina Navratilova
Monti Spry/Rob Taggart, 1978
Courtesy of Getty Images

Martina Navratilova

(b.1956)

Were you thinking what I was thinking?
The tease was on the sporting world, in
abject denial until Martina Navratilova
finally came out. That principled move,
which attracted worldwide scrutiny,
cost her millions in endorsements but
convinced an adolescent boy that
one day honesty might be not just
possible but easy. My most inspiring
schoolmaster once cautioned that
if you wanted to be gay in many
professions you'd have to be twenty
per cent better than the heterosexuals.
Watching Navratilova lift a shedful of
trophies was a reminder that, happily,
this wasn't always too difficult.

Joe Orton
Lewis Morley, 1965
National Portrait Gallery,
London (NPG P512(16))

Joe Orton
(1933–67)

The farceur who joyed in teasing the enemies of progress, Joe Orton was one of my few true childhood role models. Orton's deep mistrust of the police, church and government was heart-warming. By putting on our own school performance of *The Erpingham Camp* (1966) – 'I didn't make the rules, Chief Redcoat Riley. I only carry them out' – he gave us our own chance to poke fun too. His battiest creation was the spluttering Edna Welthorpe (Mrs). She corresponded regularly with the *Daily Telegraph* bemoaning lax morals in the 1950s and 1960s, and was spookily reincarnated two decades later with the arrival of Baroness Young in the House of Lords.

Ian Roberts
(b.1965)

Ian Roberts challenged one of the last taboos of male heterosexuality when, in 1995, he announced in the middle of a successful rugby league career that he was gay. The news from Australia was reported around the world. Not fitting the stereotypical view of how gay people act, his courageous move remains an iconic moment for many young gay men. He went on to distinguish himself as one of rugby league's great players, happily introducing his partner both to fans and fellow players.

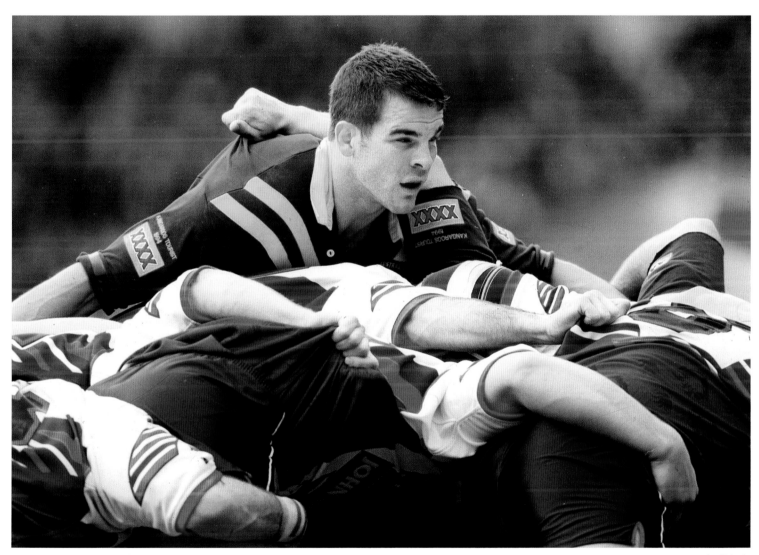

Ian Roberts
Getty Images, 1994
Courtesy of Getty Images

Sandi Toksvig

Danish comedienne, actress and writer Sandi Toksvig was born in Copenhagen, Denmark, in 1958. She studied law and anthropology at Girton College and, while at Cambridge, wrote and performed the first all-woman show at the Cambridge Footlights. Toksvig began her acting career with a season at the Nottingham Playhouse, and the New Shakespeare Company at Regent's Park. She has written both plays and musicals for the theatre, published three novels, several travel books and many children's books including *Girls Are Best*, a history book for girls. She is a columnist for the *Sunday Telegraph* and *Good Housekeeping* magazine and can be heard regularly on many BBC Radio 4 programmes, most notably as the presenter of the travel programme *Excess Baggage*, and host of *The News Quiz*. Toksvig was named Political Humorist of the Year in 2007 at the Channel 4 Political Awards and Radio Broadcaster of the Year by the Broadcasting Press Guild. In 2008 she was named Broadcaster of the Year at the Stonewall Awards.

Sandi Toksvig
Mary McCartney, 2008
National Portrait Gallery, London
© Mary McCartney

k.d. lang
Jill Furmanovsky, 1992
Jill Furmanovsky/www.rockarchive.com

k.d. lang
(b.1961)

The singer k.d. lang seemed at first a reluctant icon for the gay world. Lesbians had long adopted her as one of their own before she came out in 1992. Her anxiety that the country and western world would shun her proved unfounded. Indeed, Nashville had more trouble with her vegetarianism than her sexuality. Her sultry voice has earned her many awards in the music industry and a star on Canada's Walk of Fame. However, it is her androgynous good looks and tendency to strut on the stage that warms many lesbian hearts.

Hilda Matheson

(1888–1940)

Hilda Matheson was the first director of the BBC's Talks Department. For those of us who love BBC Radio 4 it is hard to imagine there was a time when the style of speech radio had not yet been established. Hilda had played a critical part in the development of MI5 during the First World War. In 1926 she was recruited to develop speech radio. She did so with tremendous energy, laying the foundations for the sound that is so familiar today. Matheson was the first woman to write a book about broadcasting (*Broadcasting*, 1933) and she was responsible for the *African Survey*, a mammoth research study on British colonial policy, even though Sir Malcolm (later Lord) Hailey took all the credit. She was Vita Sackville-West's lover.

Hilda Matheson
Howard Coster, 1920s
Private Collection

In 1984 Jane Cholmeley (with Sue Butterworth) put her money where her mouth was and opened Silver Moon, a feminist and lesbian bookshop in the heart of London's bookselling street, Charing Cross Road. For seventeen years she dealt with hate mail, death threats, a knife attack, flashers and general abuse to bring women the books they wanted to read. It was a safe haven where Jane often acted as much as a social worker as a bookseller. Those of us who spoke at authors' evenings remember a welcome like no other. How I miss popping in to ask her for my essential holiday reads.

Jane Cholmeley
(b.1948)

Jane Cholmeley (right; Sue Butterworth left)
Unknown photographer, 1997
Private Collection

Rosa Bonheur

(1822–99)

Rosa Bonheur was probably the most famous woman painter of the nineteenth century. She was a feisty soul, spending a considerable amount of her childhood being expelled from various schools. Her art often involved livestock as models and the finished work was much admired by Queen Victoria. What the Queen might have made of the painter's private life is hard to say. No one ever referred to Rosa as a lesbian in her day but certainly she had a 'Boston marriage', living for fifty years with her best friend Nathalie Micas. After Micas died, Rosa lived the last year of her life with the American painter Anna Elizabeth Klumpke. Rosa gained much notoriety from her application to the prefect of police to be allowed to wear trousers when she was working. 'I was forced to recognise that the clothing of my sex was a constant bother,' she said as she puffed away on a cigarette.

Rosa Bonheur
Disdéri, c.1858
National Portrait Gallery,
London (NPG Ax17185)

Peter Tatchell
(b.1952)

Peter Tatchell looks an unlikely hero. He is slight and quietly spoken yet he is one of the bravest men I have ever met. His campaigns as part of the gay activist group OutRage! have so incensed the government that they have struggled to find laws to contain him. His prosecutions have included charges under the *Ecclesiastical Courts Jurisdiction Act* and arrest under the *Terrorism Act* for displaying a banner at the wedding of Prince Charles and Camilla Parker Bowles reading 'Charles can marry twice! Gays can't marry once.' His attempts to arrest Robert Mugabe put the rest of the world to shame.

Peter Tatchell
Polly Borland, 1999
National Portrait Gallery,
London (NPG x88486)

Gene Robinson
(b.1947)

Gene Robinson is such a gentle man of God that even atheists like myself find comfort in his presence. He is funny, kind and openly loves his partner of twenty years, Mark Andrew. Yet when he was ordained as Bishop of New Hampshire in 2003 he did so wearing a bulletproof vest beneath his ceremonial robes. In a world where rape is a common tool of oppression, where millions are starving and children are abandoned, the Anglican church has decided to focus its attention on homosexuality. Gene is under constant death threats yet he carries on as living proof that the core of Christianity is supposed to be love.

Bishop Gene Robinson
Shaun Curry, 2008
Courtesy of Getty Images

Sarah Waters Born in Wales in 1966, Sarah Waters went to school locally before going to university in Canterbury. Her four novels published between 1998 and 2006 have earned her many accolades, including the Sunday Times Young Writer of the Year Award, the Somerset Maugham Award, and Author of the Year in the 2003 British Book Awards. In addition, she was named one of Granta's Twenty Best of Young British Writers, also in 2003. Waters' first novels were set in Victorian London and were inspired by her Ph.D. thesis on lesbian historical fiction. *Tipping the Velvet* (1998), *Affinity* (1999) and *Fingersmith* (2002) have been adapted for television. *Fingersmith* and *The Night Watch* (2006) were both shortlisted for the Man Booker Prize and the Orange Prize. Her latest novel is *The Little Stranger* (2009).

Denton Welch
Unknown photographer, undated
Harry Ransom Center,
The University of Texas at Austin

Denton Welch
(1915–48)

As a painter and fiction writer, Denton
Welch had a brilliantly precise and
original style. But it is his private
writings that move and impress me
most, notably the journals he kept
during the thirteen years of ill health
(as a result of suffering a fractured
spine after being hit by a car) that
preceded his early death. His life
during those years was that of a
semi-invalid, but the journals reveal
his passion for detail, for collection
and for observation; they chart his
fascination with strapping young men,
and his enduring romantic attachment
to his friend Eric Oliver. Altogether,
they form a striking, idiosyncratic
record of 1940s British life.

Patricia Highsmith
(1921–95)

Patricia Highsmith is a significant writer by any standard, but she deserves honouring as a lesbian and gay icon on the strength of one novel alone, *The Price of Salt* (1951), a wonderfully complex and upbeat representation of lesbian love, made all the more remarkable for being produced at a time when most mainstream gay narratives ended with their deviant protagonists being ruined, ridiculed, maimed, married or killed off. But much of Highsmith's later fiction, too, has a seductive homoerotic edge – in particular the psychological thrillers that feature her most memorable creation, the dangerous and decidedly queer Tom Ripley.

Bryher
Unknown photographer, undated
Beinecke Rare Book and
Manuscript Library, Yale University

Bryher
(1894–1983)

If she is remembered at all today, it is usually in relation to her long-term lover, the poet Hilda Doolittle; but I've always found Bryher herself (pen name of the writer Annie Winifred Ellerman) the more endearing figure – partly, I'm ashamed to say, simply because of her mannish good looks. But Bryher's life was an inspiring one. She was generous with her wealth, a committed patron of experimental fiction and film, and an active anti-fascist. The historical novels she wrote in the 1950s and 1960s reflect her politics, exploring the underside of recorded history by concentrating on the lives of the dispossessed, the invaded, the vulnerable and the young.

Daphne Du Maurier
Clifford Coffin, 1946
Courtesy of Condé Nast Archive

Daphne Du Maurier had secret, passionate relationships with women throughout her life and though none of her novels and short stories are explicitly lesbian, it seems to me that all of her writing is distinctly 'queer' in one way or another. Works such as *Rebecca* (1938) and *My Cousin Rachel* (1951), in particular, openly celebrate the lure and danger of powerful females. As a writer, Du Maurier inspires me in many ways. I love her storytelling skills, and her evocations of mood and place; most of all I admire her ability to create literary motifs so memorable and lasting they've entered mainstream culture with a life all their own.

Daphne Du Maurier
(1907–89)

Sylvia Townsend Warner
Howard Coster, 1934
National Portrait Gallery,
London (NPG x3370)

Sylvia Townsend Warner
(1893–1978)

It baffles and bothers me that Sylvia
Townsend Warner isn't better known
today, for she was one of the greatest
British writers of the twentieth century,
highly regarded in her own lifetime and
a prolific producer of novels, short
stories, article and poems – some of
which, notably *Mr Fortune's Maggot*
(1927) and *Summer Will Show* (1936),
have a clear homoerotic subtext. She's
an icon of mine, however, not just for
her writing, but because of her lifelong
left-wing political commitment – and also
for her passionate, moving relationship
with Valentine Ackland, her lover,
companion and comrade for almost
forty years.

Kenneth Williams
Jones, 1980
Courtesy of Getty Images

Kenneth Williams
(1926–88)

As a child in the 1970s I absolutely loved seeing Kenneth Williams on television. Perhaps it was a nascent form of gay identification on my part, for it seems to me now that the very things that appealed to me in him – his wit, his theatricality, the way his posh and fastidious manner could make sudden startling swoops into rudeness – are the very essence of camp, part of a much wider tradition of queer humour. I was sorry, as an adult, to discover what an unhappy man he was, how ill at ease with his own sexuality. He's still a comic hero of mine, wonderfully talented and fun.

ILLUSTRATION LIST

We are grateful to all those who have kindly agreed to make their photographs available for reproduction in this catalogue. The names of the owners and lenders to the exhibition, where known, are cited in the captions; the copyright holders are listed below in addition.

Every effort has been made to obtain permission from copyright holders. We apologise for any inadvertent omissions, which will be corrected in future editions if written notification is given to the publisher.

Page 12
Oscar Wilde
Napoleon Sarony, 1882
National Portrait Gallery, London (NPG P25)
© National Portrait Gallery, London

Page 13 (above)
Henry Wriothesley, 3rd Earl of Southampton
After Daniel Mytens, c.1618?
National Portrait Gallery, London (NPG 52)
© National Portrait Gallery, London

Page 13 (below)
The Ladies of Llangollen
James Henry Lynch, 1887
National Portrait Gallery, London (NPG D14047)
Bequeathed by Frederick Leverton Harris, 1927
© National Portrait Gallery, London

Page 14
Radclyffe Hall
Howard Coster, 1932
National Portrait Gallery, London (NPG x10422)
© National Portrait Gallery, London

Page 15 (above)
Richard I ('the Lionheart')
Probably by Renold or Reginold Elstrack (Elstracke), 1618
National Portrait Gallery, London (NPG D32012)
© National Portrait Gallery, London

Page 15 (below)
Queen Anne
Sir Godfrey Kneller, Bt, c.1690
National Portrait Gallery, London (NPG 1616)
© National Portrait Gallery, London

Page 16
Una, Lady Troubridge
Romaine Brooks, 1924
Smithsonian American Art Museum
© 2004 Photo Smithsonian American Art Museum/Art Resource/Scala, Florence

Page 17
Elizabeth Carter
Sir Thomas Lawrence, 1788–9
National Portrait Gallery, London (NPG 28)
© National Portrait Gallery, London

Page 19
Dame Shirley Bassey
Mike Owen, 1997
National Portrait Gallery, London (NPG x128532)
Given by Mike Owen, 2006
© Mike Owen/National Portrait Gallery, London

Page 20
Rudolf Nureyev
Cecil Beaton, 1962
National Portrait Gallery, London (NPG x40301)
Given by executors of the Estate of Eileen Hose, 1991
© Cecil Beaton Archive, Sotheby's London

Page 21
Julian Clary
Trevor Leighton, 1998
National Portrait Gallery, London (NPG x87779)
Given by Trevor Leighton, 1998
© Trevor Leighton/National Portrait Gallery, London

Page 29
Lord Waheed Alli
Mary McCartney, 2008
National Portrait Gallery, London
© Mary McCartney

Page 30
Village People
CBS Photo Archive, 1977
Courtesy of Getty Images
© 1977 Getty Images. Photo by CBS Photo Archive/Contributor/Getty Images

Page 31
Jeff Stryker
Unique hand-painted photograph
Pierre et Gilles, 1991
Courtesy Galerie Jérôme de Noirmont
© Pierre et Gilles

Page 32
Lily Savage
Paul Massey, 2003
Camera Press, London
Photograph by Paul Massey, Camera Press, London

Page 33
David Hockney
Peter Macdiarmid, 2005
Courtesy of Getty Images
© 2005 Getty Images. Photo by Peter Macdiarmid/Getty Images

Page 34
Diana, Princess of Wales
Terence Donovan, 1986
National Portrait Gallery, London (NPG P716(1))
Given by the photographer's widow, Diana Donovan, 1998
The Terence Donovan Archive, courtesy of Diana Donovan

Page 35
Will Young
Alan Olley, 2003
Camera Press, London
© Alan Olley

Page 36
Alan Hollinghurst

Mary McCartney, 2008
National Portrait Gallery, London
© Mary McCartney

Page 38
Joe Dallesandro
Paul Morrissey, 1968
Private Collection
© Paul Morrisey, 1968

Page 39
Ronald Firbank
Bertram Park, 1917
Camera Press, London
© estate of Bertram Park/Camera Press

Page 40
Gerard Manley Hopkins
Hills & Saunders, probably by George Giberne, 1863
National Portrait Gallery, London (NPG P452)
© National Portrait Gallery, London

Page 41
Edmund White
Marion Ettlinger, 2000
© Marion Ettlinger

Page 42
Pyotr Ilyich Tchaikovsky
Unknown photographer, 1890
Courtesy of Getty Images

Page 43
Thom Gunn
Rollie McKenna, 1957
© Copyright of the Estate of Rosalie Thorne McKenna

Page 45
Sir Elton John
Sam Taylor Wood, 2006
© Sam Taylor-Wood

Page 46
Gianni Versace
Andy Warhol, 1980
The Andy Warhol Museum, Pittsburgh; Contribution The Andy Warhol Foundation for the Visual Arts, Inc.
© The Andy Warhol Foundation for the Visual Arts/GreenLight, LLC

Page 47
John Lennon
Linda McCartney, 1968
National Portrait Gallery, London (NPG P575)
Given by the photographer, Linda McCartney, 1994
© 1968 estate of Linda McCartney

Page 48
Mstislav Rostropovich
Lord Snowdon, 1991
Camera Press, London
© Lord Snowdon

Page 49
Bernie Taupin
Terry O'Neill, 1975
Courtesy the photographer
© Terry O'Neill

Page 50
Graham Taylor
Mark Lawrence, 1992
Mark Lawrence/Rex Features

Page 51
Winifred Atwell
Unknown photographer, c.1950s
Courtesy of Getty Images
© c.1950 Getty Images. Photo by Popperfoto/Contributor/Getty Images

Page 53
Jackie Kay
Mary McCartney, 2008
National Portrait Gallery, London
© Mary McCartney

Page 54
Quentin Crisp
Fergus Greer, 1989
National Portrait Gallery, London (NPG x126805)
Given by Fergus Greer, 2006
© Fergus Greer

Page 55
Audre Lorde
Colleen McKay, c.1980s
Courtesy the photographer
© Colleen McKay

Page 56
Edwin Morgan

Colin Mearns, 2008
Courtesy of *The Herald*
Picture Archive –
Glasgow
Image by Colin Mearns
courtesy of *The Herald*
Picture Archive –
Glasgow

Page 57
Bessie Smith
Unknown photographer,
c.1920s
Courtesy of Getty
Images
© 1925 Getty Images.
Photo by Frank Driggs/
Getty Images

Page 58
Billy Tipton
Unknown photographer,
1951
Private Collection
© reserved

Page 59
Sojourner Truth
Unknown photographer,
1864
Courtesy of the Library
of Congress, ppmsca
08979

Page 60
Billie Jean King
Mary McCartney, 2008
National Portrait Gallery,
London
© Mary McCartney

Page 62
The Moffitt Family
Unknown photographer,
c.1970s
Private Collection

Page 63
Ilana Kloss
Unknown photographer,
2009
Courtesy of Getty
Images
© 2009 Getty Images

Page 64
Christiane Amanpour
Brent Stirton, 2007
© Brent Stirton/Getty
Images for CNN

Page 65
Althea Gibson
Reg Birkett/Douglas
Miller, 1958

Courtesy of Getty
Images
© 1958 Getty Images.
Photo by Keystone/
Stringer/Getty Images

Page 66
Nelson Mandela
Ian Berry, 1994
Ian Berry/Magnum
Photos

Page 67
Reverend Bob Richards
Unknown photographer,
1952
IOC Olympic Museum
Collections
© CIO/Lothar Rübelt

Page 69
Sir Ian McKellen
Mary McCartney, 2008
National Portrait Gallery,
London
© Mary McCartney

Page 70
Margarethe
Cammermeyer
Andreea Dragomir, 2008
Grethe Cammermeyer
© Grethe Cammermeyer

Page 71
Edward Carpenter
Alfred Mattison, copied
by Emery Walker Ltd,
1905
National Portrait Gallery,
London (NPG x87106)
Given by Emery Walker
Ltd, 1956
© National Portrait
Gallery, London

Page 72
H.I.H. Regina Fong
Unknown photographer,
2003
Private Collection

Page 73
Angela Mason
Maggie Murray for
Format Photographers,
1999
National Portrait Gallery,
London (NPG x132183)
© Maggie Murray/
National Portrait Gallery,
London

Page 74
Harvey Milk

Efren Convento Ramirez,
1978
Courtesy the
photographer
© Efren Ramirez,
1978/2008

Page 75
Walt Whitman
Attributed to Gabriel
Harrison, c.1850s
Rare Books Division,
The New York Public
Library, Astor, Lenox
and Tilden Foundations

Page 77
Lord Chris Smith
Mary McCartney, 2008
National Portrait Gallery,
London
© Mary McCartney

Page 78
Edwin Cameron
Piers Allardyce, 2005
Courtesy the
photographer
© Piers Allardyce

Page 79
W.H. Auden
Cecil Beaton, 1967
National Portrait Gallery,
London (NPG x40007)
Given by executors of
the Estate of Eileen
Hose, 1991
© Cecil Beaton Archive,
Sotheby's London

Page 80
Benjamin Britten, Baron
Britten
Cecil Beaton, 1942
National Portrait Gallery,
London (NPG x14036)
Given by Cecil Beaton,
1968
© Cecil Beaton Archive,
Sotheby's London

Page 81
John Menlove Edwards
Geoffrey Bartrum,
c.1930s
Private Collection
© reserved

Page 82
Virginia Woolf
Gisèle Freund, 1939
National Portrait Gallery,
London (NPG P440)
© Gisèle Freund

Page 83
Alan Turing
Elliott and Fry, 1951
National Portrait Gallery,
London (NPG x82217)
© National Portrait
Gallery, London

Page 85
Ben Summerskill
Mary McCartney, 2008
National Portrait Gallery,
London
© Mary McCartney

Page 86
Maya Angelou
Michael Ochs Archive,
1970
Courtesy of Getty
Images
© 1970 Getty Images.
Photo by Michael Ochs
Archives/Stringer/Getty
Images

Page 87
Ellen DeGeneres
Michael Thompson,
2005
Courtesy the
photographer

Page 88
Francis Bacon
John Hedgecoe, 1970
National Portrait Gallery,
London (NPG P158)
© John Hedgecoe

Page 89
Martina Navratilova
Monti Spry/Rob Taggart,
1978
Courtesy of Getty
Images
© 1978 Getty Images.
Photo by Central Press/
Stringer/Getty Images

Page 90
Joe Orton
Lewis Morley, 1965
National Portrait Gallery,
London (NPG P512(16))
Given by the
photographer, Lewis
Morley, 1992
© Lewis Morley Archive/
National Portrait Gallery,
London

Page 91
Ian Roberts
Getty Images, 1994

Courtesy of Getty
Images
© 1994 Getty Images.
Photo by Getty Images/
staff

Page 93
Sandi Toksvig
Mary McCartney, 2008
National Portrait Gallery,
London
© Mary McCartney

Page 94
k.d. lang
Jill Furmanovsky, 1992
© Jill Furmanovsky/
www.rockarchive.com

Page 95
Hilda Matheson
Howard Coster, 1920s
Private Collection

Page 96
Jane Cholmeley
Unknown photographer,
1997
Private Collection
Courtesy *The Bookseller*

Page 97
Rosa Bonheur
Disdéri, c.1858
National Portrait Gallery,
London (NPG Ax17185)
Given by Algernon
Graves, 1916
© National Portrait
Gallery, London

Page 98
Peter Tatchell
Polly Borland, 1999
National Portrait Gallery,
London (NPG x88486)
© Polly Borland

Page 99
Bishop Gene Robinson
Shaun Curry, 2008
Courtesy of Getty
Images
© 2008 Getty Images.
Photo by Shaun
Curry/Stringer/Getty
Images

Page 101
Sarah Waters
Mary McCartney,
2008
National Portrait Gallery,
London
© Mary McCartney

Page 102
Denton Welch
Unknown photographer,
undated
Harry Ransom Center,
The University of Texas
at Austin

Page 103
Patricia Highsmith
Harper & Brothers, 1962
Patricia Highsmith
Collection, Swiss
National Library/Swiss
Literary Archives, Bern
© Patricia Highsmith
Collection, Swiss
National Library/Swiss
Literary Archives, Bern

Page 104
Bryher
Unknown photographer,
undated
Beinecke Rare Book
and Manuscript Library,
Yale University

Page 105
Daphne Du Maurier
Clifford Coffin, 1946
Courtesy of Condé
Nast Archive
© Condé Nast
Publications

Page 106
Sylvia Townsend Warner
Howard Coster, 1934
National Portrait Gallery,
London (NPG x3370)
© National Portrait
Gallery, London

Page 107
Kenneth Williams
Jones, 1980
Courtesy of Getty
Images
© 1980 Getty Images.
Photo by Evening
Standard/Stringer/
Getty Images

INDEX